THE WAY OF BEATITUDE

"In *The Way of Beatitude*, Fr. Casey Cole, OFM, challenges us to encounter the Beatitudes in a new and hopeful manner. His fresh perspective is insightful, humorous, and practical. The examples from life experience and thought-provoking questions make this an excellent guide to pursuing and living the Beatitudes in one's own life."

Bishop Michael F. Burbidge
Diocese of Arlington

"What a great book! Fr. Casey Cole, OFM, offers a beautiful and deep encounter with the Beatitudes. By offering a contemplative approach that nurtures a lived response to Jesus, he helps us encounter the poverty of spirit that ought to fill the heart of every person."

Fr. Harrison Ayre
Cohost of the *Clerically Speaking* podcast

"Few can reach across the divides of our Church and world— age, ideology, clerical state—like Fr. Casey Cole. He brings the wisdom of the gospels into the twenty-first century and models how we can be agents of peace in a polarized age."

Ashley McKinless
Executive editor at *America*
Cohost of the *Jesuitical* podcast

"A contemporary, wonderfully realistic look at the Beatitudes by one of Catholicism's most positive voices. Franciscan Fr. Casey Cole breathes new life into these sayings of Jesus by coupling them with personal stories of lessons learned and practical ways to engage with them yourself."

Mike Hayes
Cofounder of Busted Halo

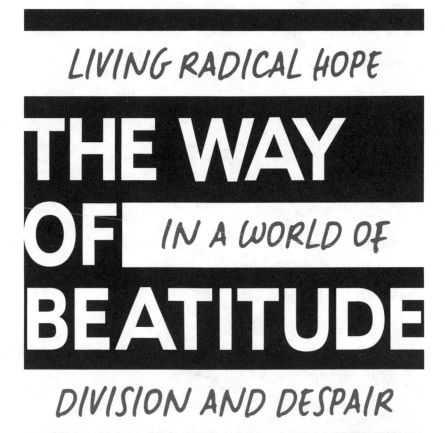

LIVING RADICAL HOPE

THE WAY
OF
IN A WORLD OF
BEATITUDE

DIVISION AND DESPAIR

CASEY COLE, OFM

AVE MARIA PRESS AVE Notre Dame, Indiana

Founded in 1865, Ave Maria Press is a ministry of the United States Province of Holy Cross.

www.avemariapress.com

Paperback: ISBN-13 978-1-64680-145-9

E-book: ISBN-13 978-1-64680-146-6

Cover and text design by Samantha Watson.

Printed and bound in the United States of America.

Library of Congress Cataloging-in-Publication Data
Names: Cole, Casey, author.
Title: The way of beatitude : living radical hope in a world of division
  and despair / Casey Cole, OFM.
Description: Notre Dame, Indiana : Ave Maria Press, 2022. | Summary: "In
  this book, Casey Cole writes about the necessity of the Beatitudes for
  Christian life. He uses simple reflections from his own life to invite
  the reader to meditate on the Beatitudes along with him"-- Provided by
  publisher.
Identifiers: LCCN 2021054413 (print) | LCCN 2021054414 (ebook) | ISBN
  9781646801459 (paperback) | ISBN 9781646801466 (ebook)
Subjects: LCSH: Beatitudes--Criticism, interpretation, etc. | Bible.
  Matthew, V, 3-12--Criticism, interpretation, etc.
Classification: LCC BT382 .C63 2022 (print) | LCC BT382 (ebook) | DDC
  241.5/3--dc23/eng/20211130
LC record available at https://lccn.loc.gov/2021054413
LC ebook record available at https://lccn.loc.gov/2021054414

CONTENTS

INTRODUCTION

It's no secret that our world has become more polarized in recent years. Many people had great hope that the proliferation of the internet and social communication would unify the world by instantly and universally disseminating facts and dispelling rumors. Sadly, while people are more closely connected and the sharing of information, knowledge, and our daily lives has greatly enhanced aspects of contemporary life, the opposite has also been the case: the democratization and expansion of media has also further divided us—or at least exposed and amplified our divisions. While social media and twenty-four-hour news cycles could offer a fruitful exchange of ideas and the positive expansion of our worldview, much of our experience is instead fraught with controversy and divisive exchanges. We cringe when we look at our news feeds and see what our friends and family members are posting about religion, politics, and society; we bubble with anger at what pundits are saying about the things we know and love; we deflate with exhaustion at the never-ending battles.

For some, the natural response to a divided world is to double down on division. If they want a fight, then they are going to get a fight! Emboldened by their own stance, and convinced of their enemy's error, many engage in the so-called "culture wars" by consuming as much toxicity as they can and taking up arms. Enemies are judged and condemned, attacks are waged. It's important, they believe, that those in error not only know of their error but experience some level of shame as a result of being so wrong. The truth must be spoken regardless of how anyone feels. More times than not, this leads to further division.

Others view these exchanges as entirely futile but also struggle to see a way to achieve anything of worth. They become convinced that no one will ever change their mind and all that's really gained by interacting with those with whom they disagree is resentment. The world is divided and always will be divided. Rather than outrage, they feel a deepening sense of helplessness at the direction the human family seems to be going. Too often, this perception leads to despair or apathy.

Neither of these approaches is particularly hopeful or particularly novel to our time. Two thousand years ago, the world faced many of the same kinds of ills and divisions that we do today. In Jesus's time, the poor were oppressed, the powerful reigned, the greedy took advantage, and violence served as the purest form of order. People unhappy with their current circumstances had the choice to return violence with violence—a choice that most certainly ensured their own death—or to keep their heads down and out of the way—a choice that most certainly ensured a life of misery. The world was corrupt, and there was little one could do about it.

But something changed with Jesus. His preaching offered a different perspective; his very existence offered an opportunity for hope. While he is often viewed by the world as a man with a strong moral message, someone who went to bad people to make them good, we as Christians know that his mission was one of liberation. He went to the hopeless, poor, oppressed people of the world, not to tell them that they were bad, but to free them from all that held them captive. He came to bring life. The great mystery of the Incarnation is not so much that

God now has a human voice to teach and hands to heal, but that humanity now has within itself the ability to partake in the divine life of the Trinity. In taking on human flesh, dying, and rising again, Jesus made it possible for us to rise and be blessed. That's the beauty of the Paschal Mystery that we celebrate. Like the landlord in the parable of the talents (see Matthew 25:14–30), Jesus's life and mission seem to shout, "Come, share in your master's joy! Come, share in the blessedness of God!"

This is the invitation of the Beatitudes. What Jesus offers to the hopeless, poor, oppressed people of his time is a third option. Rather than respond with violence or give in to despair, he shows us a path to true blessedness. For many it is the life that they already know. For Jesus, there is something about poverty, mourning, meekness, hunger, mercy, purity, peace, and persecution that not only prepares one for the future reality of the kingdom of heaven, but makes one blessed in the here and now. He does not say that those who experience these things *will* be blessed, but that they *are* blessed. By virtue of their experience, because of the qualities they possess, they find themselves already partakers in the divine life.

The Beatitudes offer great hope, enabling the downtrodden and excluded to endure the divisiveness of the world until they can receive in fullness the reward of the kingdom of heaven. I hope that this book will serve as such for you as well, reminding you—or helping you see for the first time—that, despite our present difficulties, a better future awaits. But the insight I try to offer in this book extends beyond that. Given the specific situation we face, I would like to argue that the Beatitudes do more than just pacify us for the future; they provide us with opportunities to partake in the divine life here and now. That is, they offer a path toward radical change in the present. Jesus tells us that the kingdom of heaven is at hand; the blessedness of God is inbreaking, transforming the world around us. We need not resort to violence or cower in despair. Those who live in God and have God living in them can offer the world a third option: the way of Beatitude.

1. SURRENDER

BLESSED ARE THE POOR IN SPIRIT

> Blessed are the poor in spirit, for theirs is the kingdom of heaven.
>
> —Matthew 5:3

God Is Enough

When I was in college, I worked one summer at a church in a poor part of Greenville, South Carolina. The houses in the neighborhood were small and run-down, the tenants poor and struggling. I was shocked that some people lived without running water in their homes. They filled buckets from an outside hose or from the neighboring fire department and carried it inside to shower, use the bathroom, and take care of other daily needs. Many were not only unemployed but unemployable, coming to the church's food pantry each week in desperate need. Had they shown up at our door angry and rude, I would have completely understood why. They had no money, no jobs, no comfort, no safety, and no social status to speak of. By earthly standards, their lives were dreadful.

And yet, most of these people didn't think that their lives were dreadful. Very few complained. Many of them were incredibly friendly, optimistic people who enjoyed life. They smiled when I greeted them, laughed freely and loudly, sat and talked as though I was a long-lost friend. There was no doubt that many of them were coping with serious issues, but by and large, they believed they lived blessed lives.

In Macon, Georgia, where I live today, there is a man I've come to know at the homeless day center who typifies my experiences from that summer in college. Highly intelligent and pleasant to talk to, if you were to meet him on the street knowing nothing about him, you'd think that he was a teacher or counselor at a school. In fact, he was for many years. Unfortunately, because of mental health issues, he can no longer maintain a job or take care of his life as he once could, and he's landed where so many end up—living on the streets, forced to sleep under a bridge. He relies on the center for food, showers, laundry, and basic medical attention. Surely not a situation in which many could find hope.

But ask him how he's doing in the morning, and his answer will always be the same: "I'm blessed, Father, truly blessed." He reads the Bible daily, prays constantly, and is one of the most positive, dedicated people you'll ever meet. He believes with his entire being that his life is a gift from God to be shared. At the center, he doesn't just take what he needs; he volunteers his time as a reliable member of the staff, seven days a week. He sees that his entire life is filled with gifts from God and that he has something to provide others on the streets—that being homeless isn't as much an affliction to escape as it is an opportunity to serve others. It's through his experience of poverty that he has come to love God and neighbor in a way that stability and comfort never would allow.

When I say that his story is similar to those of others I've encountered, that's not an exaggeration. His life is an incredible witness of how God is enough, that even those with absolutely nothing can feel satisfied when they have faith. Starting that summer in college but continuing throughout my life as a friar, I have met hosts of people in multiple countries around the world who exhibit the same level of faith despite their humble means. It is because of this that many have argued that it is not *despite* their poverty that their faith is so strong, but entirely *because* of it. Many are convinced that the poor have stronger faith.

Of course, this perspective does not apply to all of the poor. For as true as it is that great faith can exist even when money doesn't, there are also plenty of people suffering from poverty who want nothing to do with God, who curse God and neighbor for what they have to deal with. Some may not mind living under a bridge or walking to the fire station in order to flush the toilet, but most find those things dehumanizing. They want a bed. They don't think it's too much to ask that every person be afforded a working toilet to use. Gradually beaten down by these serious grievances, they find themselves with no time for God. The poor do not all have faith because they're poor—some are just as hopeless, mean, greedy, and evil as anyone else. I've met plenty of them.

I regularly encounter another man at the homeless center who, I believe, has never once smiled in his whole life. He walks in with a frown on his face, shoulders tensed, ready to pick a fight with someone. As far as I'm concerned, he is not just unpleasant to be around, he's vicious. On numerous occasions I have found myself the recipient of one of his cutting remarks because I didn't recall how he liked his coffee from the last time I served him—a week earlier with more than fifty coffee orders between. Rather than just saying what he wants when I politely ask him, he launches into a tirade about how I'm incompetent for not remembering, insulting me and the center. (Although, to be fair, if his goal was to get me to be so afraid that I would remember his order next time, it worked. I'm not sure I will *ever* forget it.)

To receive treatment like this was nothing unusual if you spent any time working at the friars' soup kitchen in Philadelphia, as I did during another summer in college. While some of those we served touched me with their kindness and faith, quite a few more left an impact on me for being just awful people. One time, an employee literally saved a man from overdosing on drugs, springing to action with a naloxone shot when he lost consciousness; once revived, the man did not thank the employee but tried to attack him for ruining his high. When there are enough volunteers, one person is assigned to watch the bathrooms, as people will come in each day to steal the industrial-sized rolls of toilet paper, take a shower using the sink, or leave the bathroom entirely trashed and unusable for others. There are people who bring weapons into the dining room, threatening the staff or guests. And while it's not a frequent occurrence, we occasionally have to add a name to our list of the "permanently banned . . . for the time being." "Permanently banned" because they are a menace to society that can't be safely admitted, and "for the time being" because we're Franciscans and no one is beyond mercy.

That is simply the reality of poverty. Some of the poor have wonderful faith, yes, but others are absolutely wretched. People who live in poverty have just as much free will as the rest of us to be good or bad, to follow God or not.

Because of the wonderful people that feel blessed despite their poverty, there can be a tendency to romanticize poverty itself as a blessed condition, to make destitution into a sort of virtue, and so believe that God loves poverty or desires it. Yet this is simply not the case. While scripture tells us that the materially poor do have a special place in God's heart—that he hears their cries, answers their prayers, identifies with them, and will always end up on their side—it is also true that in scripture poverty is always treated as an *affliction*. It is an experience of evil. Material, involuntary poverty is not the product of God's will but of humanity's greed. The suffering that humanity experiences as a result of poverty is not something that brings joy in itself, and being poor is no automatic ticket to heaven. To believe this might lead some to read the first Beatitude as declaring charity and justice unnecessary, that the poor should endure their suffering quietly or that God somehow desires destitution. None of these things are true.

When Jesus refers to the poor as blessed, he does not refer to the condition itself, as if destitution was a good to be sought, but rather to the opportunity the materially poor have in their spiritual lives. Because poverty strips people of material comfort, a sense of safety, and all too often the simple grace of being treated with dignity, the poor may find themselves more readily disposed to face the futility that life throws their way. The poor often know how to ask for help, while the rich may be too proud. The people I met at the food pantry knew that they were not capable of taking care of themselves, that their own abilities were not enough; they knew what human weakness got them, and so looked to the last place left to offer help. Many of those people knew what rock bottom feels like, that there is nowhere else to go but to God. In this way, the poor can find themselves more readily predisposed to God, not because of what they have—suffering, oppression, anxiety—but because of what they don't have: arrogance, self-sufficiency, or, frankly, other options. Unlike the rich and comfortable, the poor are too often forced to see that there is no hope in anything but God, that if they want to survive, they must choose him above all else. In this there is blessing. But they still have to choose. We all do.

Being poor doesn't give someone a ticket to heaven in the same way that being rich doesn't negate our salvation. Entry into the kingdom isn't granted based on the status of one's bank account, but by the wholehearted commitment to God's love. It's about recognizing the futility of the world and surrendering one's entire life to God, finding treasure in nothing more than the work of the Gospel. The condition of poverty offers the advantage of removing the worldly comforts that can distract us from the true source of life, but in the end, it is not about money. It's about faith. It's about dependence. It's about realizing that there is nothing in this world that could possibly offer us fulfillment if we don't have God, so what's the use in pursuing it?

When Jesus speaks of the blessedness of the poor, this is what he's talking about. When he tells his disciples that they must give up everything and follow him, this is what he wants: a complete surrender of one's life, the acceptance that human ability is nothing to God's ability. Jesus is not after suffering or destitution; he's after humility, trust, and complete dependence on God. Blessed are those who surrender completely to God, for theirs is the kingdom of heaven.

The Futility of a Self-Reliant World

A little more than a month before I wrote this, my sister gave birth to her first child. I met my first niece a few weeks later, and I have to say, she is an absolute blessing to the family. I know everyone thinks their baby is the cutest thing in the world, what with their big eyes, toothless smiles, and rolls upon rolls of fat on their legs, but nobody's baby has anything on my niece. Born ten pounds seven ounces, she is in the ninety-ninth percentile when it comes to cute, chubby babies.

As you can imagine, though, a baby that size was not the greatest blessing at the time of the delivery! She was a week late, then too big to deliver, so my sister ended up needing a C-section. It made everyone a bit anxious the day of—nobody wants complications in childbirth—but both mother and baby made it through okay and are healthy today. Although complications can always arise and giving birth is itself *never* an easy task, medicine has advanced so tremendously over the years that such a procedure is all but routine for doctors today. Our family was concerned, sure, and I offered a prayer for my sister that everything would go well, but the worry we experienced was nothing like the debilitating fear that would have consumed a family in the same situation a century ago.

Which is really quite incredible, if you think about it. In the grand scheme of human history, we're talking about a drop in the bucket, and yet the differences make it seem like a foreign world. When my grandfather was born in 1920, his mother was 800 times more likely to die in childbirth than my sister was today. He himself was more than 100 times more likely to die before the age of one than my niece. And these were no doubt advancements from previous generations. Had I been living in any other time than our own when I received word that my sister had to have surgery to deliver the baby, I would have been worried sick. Chances are the delivery itself, even under normal circumstances, would have been cause for an all-night vigil, a prayer of desperate plea to God to bring hope to something so dangerous. Safe delivery would have evoked such overwhelming joy and thanksgiving that grand sacrifices would have been offered to God. Given the risk, how could people of old *not* have seen it as the work of God?

But I didn't do any of that. I said a brief prayer prior to the surgery, offered a moment of thanksgiving that night, and moved on with my life. A baby was born, as expected. Her presence is a profound blessing, as is the now-routine surgical procedure that brought her to us and kept both her and my sister safe. The whole experience made me reflect upon things in a new way. As I think about how modern medicine has advanced, giving us such precision in our diagnoses and command over the human body, I can't help but feel emotionally disconnected from the healing stories of the Bible. The woman with hemorrhages suffered at the hands of doctors for twelve years until finding hope in Jesus; Jairus must have felt entirely helpless when his daughter died, not knowing how or why it had happened; the lepers couldn't even be around people, let alone find someone who could cure them. They all ran to Jesus because they had nowhere else to turn. They knew there was nothing they could do, nothing the world could offer, that could bring them relief. Jesus was all they could depend on.

Not so today. While I would like to make it abundantly clear that I find the advancements in modern medicine to be a tremendous gift to humanity—getting a scraped knee or paper cut and not having to worry about the possibility of death from infection is delightful!—I can't help but think we've also lost something along the way. As we continue to advance in our ability to take care of ourselves, there is a part of us that begins to think we don't actually need anyone but ourselves. However subtle or subconscious, there is a tendency to give our full trust to human endeavors, no longer needing to worry, no longer forced to pray, no longer aware of the fact that everything we do is dependent upon God's grace.

If complete surrender to God is the way to blessedness, it's no wonder our world is fragmented and fraught with controversy. Beneath the vast array of arguments and opinions that contribute to the divisiveness of our age, I believe there is but a single problem: a prideful world that trusts in itself and gives its allegiance entirely to saviors that cannot save. This can take many forms.

For some it is politics. Frustrated with the brokenness of society, increasing numbers of people are placing all their hope in politicians and social movements. It is not simply an engaged and concerned populace; it is a desperate and frenetic one. Every issue is treated as a matter of life and death; every debate an ultimatum defining one's relationships. It is as if the fate of the world depends on what a politician or news pundit says.

For others, it is a matter of lifestyle or identity markers that come to define everything. Feeling completely without control in an ever-changing, chaotic world, some have not only chosen to adopt a countercultural way of living, but have let it come to define who they are and why others are wrong. At some point, it moves beyond a personal desire for simplicity, tradition, antiquity, health, or personal aesthetic and becomes the unwavering belief—subconscious or not—that this particular lifestyle choice can solve the world's problems and bring about ultimate happiness.

For others still, it is nothing more than inflated trust in oneself. In some places, Christianity and the American spirit have become so fused that self-reliance and independence—the ability to take care of oneself without help from another—are treated as Christian values. These people rest on their abilities. They trust in the power within them to be the answer to every problem they may have, making human ingenuity their god. A being beyond reproach. A being not to be questioned. A being that deserves respect, so how dare you disagree with me?

Herein lies the problem. When one's utmost hope and identity come to rest in human ability rather than the truth of the Gospel, disagreement is no longer viewed as a mere difference of opinion but as a threat to one's god. At this point, it doesn't matter how trivial the conversation may seem, it is no longer a matter of civil discourse or philosophical debate; it is a matter of honor and supreme identity. Few will be able to tolerate this or engage their critic civilly. Rationality need not apply; compromise is out of the question. It is no wonder, then, that hurtful rhetoric appears on one's social media feed or divisive arguments arise amongst family members. A god has been attacked and one's utmost hope has been questioned. All that's left is to fight or flee, choose violence or despair.

As much as a self-reliant attitude may offer us a sense of identity that we desperately crave, it will ultimately be one that cannot offer us what we truly need. Our abilities are not enough. Our social movements are too exclusive. Our politics are too shortsighted. They may be effective for a time but ultimately provide nothing more than a false sense of security. When we put our trust in something that is not God, we stake our claim on something that cannot bring us the ultimate answer, inevitably leading to disappointment. Politicians will let us down. Movements will go out of style. Bodies will become frail. There is only One who will never let us down, who can offer us the true fulfillment of the heavenly kingdom. It is only when we put our trust in God and God alone, surrendering completely to him, that we can overcome the discord in our world, for it is only then that we can see what truly matters and what is not worth fighting over.

How do we do that? I recommend a life committed to acts of voluntary poverty. Just as some people tend to romanticize poverty as a material condition, others tend to overly spiritualize it, stripping it of any lived experience. It is the person who lives a posh life, filled with luxuries, who says, "I have all of these things, but I don't need them. I could give them up and be just as happy." That may in fact be the case, but it remains to be seen. One may have great faith and be extremely thankful, but it is difficult to be dependent when all we have is comfort. If we are to understand what it means to fully surrender to God, there must come a point in our lives when we are actually desperate, when we know we need help, and so are forced to rely on God because we have felt the futility of our own ability.

An act as simple as riding the bus instead of driving to where we need to go might be helpful in changing our attitude. When I was in seminary, I began to realize how many people relied on public transit. Feeling a bit guilty about having my own car, I decided to take the bus to school each day, no matter what, for an entire school year. I expected it to be physically uncomfortable, and it certainly was: the additional quarter-mile walk up a hill was tiring in the morning, rain and snow meant a wet habit and cold feet for hours, and the bus itself was slow, bumpy, and often overcrowded. What I did not expect, however, and what provided the far greater challenge, was the mental and emotional toll that played on me. I lived with very real stress each morning that I might be late. The ride itself was mind-numbingly boring, taking nearly an hour of my life with nothing productive to do. While I never felt unsafe, there was definitely a sense of feeling exposed, thrown together with strangers without any personal space or privacy. All told, what I experienced that year was not just discomfort, but a heavy dose of powerlessness.

I would like to suggest that this is an essential experience for all Christians. While powerlessness in itself is demoralizing and dehumanizing and may serve only to push some people further away from true freedom, the Christian seeking to surrender completely to God will recognize within it an invitation to more closely identify with the life and Passion of Christ, to imitate his self-emptying and perfect surrender to the Father's will. What made this experience fruitful for me was not the discomfort in itself, but the surrender of my will that followed and the fruit it bore. I became more patient in times of stress, grateful for what I had, and empathetic to the struggles of my poorer neighbors. Changes in perspective like this cannot be fully realized without some experience of real, material poverty.

This is why Jesus calls his disciples to be poor. To follow Jesus, we needn't sell all we have and live on the street, but we must know what it feels like to be hungry. We need to know what it's like to be powerless. We need to feel a desperation that shakes us to our core, making it so abundantly clear that we cannot survive without God that we wouldn't even think about trying. Our dependence on God must be so strong that we completely reevaluate what's considered wealth and how we interact with it; that when faced with difficulties, we are not even tempted to look to the world because we have already been relying on God through the good times; that we have come to find the world and all its allurements so futile and unreliable that we actually prefer being poor, because it is in our poverty that we find the most strength in God. When we have surrendered so completely to God that even poverty is a gift, we are on the way of Beatitude.

Questions for Reflection

1. What has your experience with the poor been like? How much time have you spent with individuals who live in poverty? What gifts have they offered you through their faith in God?

2. How much of your life is determined by your own decisions, and how much do you have to rely on others? Do you ever let others lead, knowing nothing of what you are going to do? How does that make you feel?

3. In what ways might you adopt a lifestyle of voluntary poverty?

Practical Acts of Surrender

- Go through your closet, and consider each item. Don't just ask if you like it or use it, but if it might better serve someone else. Give away the items you don't need, and if you're feeling up for a particularly serious act of surrender, maybe even a few things that you do.

- Try to incorporate a Lenten spirit of self-denial throughout the year. The Church has held the tradition for centuries that Friday is to be a day of penance in remembrance of Christ's Passion, and adopting a year-round practice might help keep that spirit alive for you. It can be as simple as abstaining from meat or spending an additional thirty minutes in prayer each Friday.

- Ask for help more often. To facilitate this practice, purposefully do something you're not good at. Let yourself be humbled by your own lack of ability and feel the powerlessness of needing to rely on someone else.

2. HEARTBREAK

BLESSED ARE THEY WHO MOURN

Blessed are they who mourn, for they will be comforted.
—Matthew 5:4

Love That Won't Quit

I served as a hospital chaplaincy intern for a time, and my role was to walk around the hospital visiting patients, talking to them about any spiritual or emotional concern they might have. At the time, I was not ordained, and to this day I am not trained to deal with trauma on a clinical level, and so my conversations were generally casual and generic. I was supposed to make people feel comfortable, help with their boredom, and maybe provide a little hope. When I arrived at the hospital one morning and heard about the new patient in pediatrics, I knew that I probably wasn't going to be able to do any of those things.

Overnight, a girl had come to the hospital, no more than twelve years old, having attempted to take her own life by overdosing on drugs. Thinking about the turmoil someone must feel to want to end their own life saddens me to my bones; to think about a child in middle school dealing with this is just unbearable. It was a tremendous tragedy that would leave anyone devastated. But her tragedy was far from over. Being so young, she didn't know what she was doing, and so the drug she chose was Tylenol, a relatively weak medication that posed little actual threat to her life, but one that can do significant damage to the liver when consumed in large doses. And so, there she was, a child that never came close to actually dying, but was left with a near-unworkable liver. She would require regular dialysis until a transplant liver was made available, if she was even eligible to receive one. Her parents were devastated but stood by their little girl, tears in their eyes, willing to do anything they could.

What was I supposed to say to them? How could I bring hope to people facing such a debilitating tragedy? Sadly, experiences such as this are not particularly extraordinary for people who frequent hospitals. Tragedies are around every corner; heartbreak abounds. Family members are forced to make heart-rending decisions about the care of a loved one; young, healthy people are given devastating diagnoses; parents have to watch as their children suffer.

Really, tragedies such as these are common enough. I think of the pain that must be felt by the thousands of people in America each year who lose a loved one to gun violence; the tens of thousands worldwide who lose a child under the age of five to preventable deaths such as accidents and treatable diseases each *day*. Migrants and refugees flee violence in war-torn areas, members of marginalized groups are subject to persecution, innumerable people are born into destitution with little hope of a long, prosperous life. Sorrow abounds for those willing to see.

It is to these people—the people of two thousand years ago and the people of our time—that Jesus preached a seemingly preposterous message: blessed are those who mourn. For anyone who thought his opening line about the poor was crazy, this one must have come off as outright nonsense. Sorrow has the ability to deaden the mind and extinguish the spirit. Tragedies can leave people feeling demoralized and broken, unsettled and depressed, unsure of how to go on. Like Mary after the death of her brother Lazarus, some may have hope in the Resurrection and so hold on to the prospect of future comfort, but it would seem impossible to find anything blessed about the situation itself. How is it that Jesus can say that these people are in any way blessed in the *now*?

As was the case with the Beatitude of poverty, I think it is important to distinguish between the conditions people encounter and the way people respond to such conditions. Just as material poverty in itself is an evil that God neither wills nor desires, so, too, are the tragedies that too many people endure. Hunger, violence, disease, betrayal, theft, abuse, death itself—at no point does Jesus say that any of these things are goods to be sought or conditions necessary for discipleship. They do not exist in the garden before sin, and they are not things that God wants for his people. Rather, what makes someone blessed is not the fact that they live with a dehumanizing affliction, it's that they *respond* to it in a holy way. In this case, the response we seek is the activity we call mourning.

To understand how significant healthy, sacred mourning is and how it can be an opportunity for blessedness, we might first think of its absence: tragedy *without* mourning. Imagine if someone received word that their spouse had died unexpectedly, that their child was diagnosed with an inoperable tumor, that they themselves were being fired and evicted from their home on the same day. Now imagine if this same person were entirely unaffected, showing absolutely no sorrow. What might you think about that person?

As much as we associate tragedy with mourning, one does not always lead to the other. For any number of reasons, some people experience great personal tragedies with little immediate response. They may find themselves in a state of denial and haven't fully processed what's happened. Maybe the pain is so raw that their mind has involuntarily shut down to protect itself. While one cannot fault another for being in shock, there is a sense, at the very least, that the reality of sorrow has not come to be fully realized and processed in these situations. To experience tragedy without mourning may save us a lot of pain, but it also seems to keep us far from the reality before us. In the long run, to never mourn a loss, even the seemingly minor losses of life, is to be less than who we are created to be.

As strange as it may sound, I think we would all prefer the person who mourns, the one who cannot see tragedy without being affected, to the person who never lets down her emotional safeguards, or never allows his heart to be broken. There are aspects of mourning—vulnerability, empathy, sorrow, tears—that make us more relatable to others and far more like God. Only in hearts that have been broken is there room for compassion, mercy, and love to grow.

When Jesus says, "Blessed are those who mourn," he does not speak of the condition of tragedy in itself, but rather of the capacity of a person to *feel*: blessed are those who care enough to cry. Blessed are those who are deeply moved by tragic events. Blessed are those who choose to love even when it would hurt a lot less *not* to love. For what does it mean to mourn other than to love in the face of loss, to persist in caring even when all seems hopeless, to refuse to move on easily or quickly from pain? When we speak of someone mourning, our focus isn't so much on the events that caused the person's sorrow as it is on the magnitude of a heart vulnerable enough to suffer with and for another. An uncaring heart does not mourn. Someone with no commitment, no vulnerability, and no self-sacrifice does not mourn. Only the one who loves, even when it hurts, is able to shed a tear. This is a blessed person.

How amazing it is, then, when someone can mourn not only for their own personal loss but for the loss of another. What does it say about a person who can cry not only for themselves, but with and for another? This is a blessed person as well, and this is why mourning together is such an important sign of a healthy Christian community. It is an experience of vulnerability that simultaneously reveals how much we care about another and allows others to care about us more deeply. There is something about crying together that binds us to one another.

I think of the times in my life that I have comforted those who were mourning and those times that others have comforted me. I once sat with a man after he learned of a death in the family. With my arm on his shoulder, he cried uncontrollably in a state of complete desolation. I had never met the deceased, nor can I say that I was particularly close to the mourner prior to this encounter, but there was something binding about that moment. Given the stigma that crying has among some people, particularly men, I can think of only a handful of moments in my life in which I felt more in communion with another person. Neither of us felt ashamed. We were connected to one another in love, sharing in each other's sorrows.

Although it was his sorrow at the time, it had been my sorrow at another time. I was able to relate to him in a time when I was experiencing no personal tragedy of my own because I had been there before. I knew the sting of loss. I knew what it felt like to be lost and broken, had shed my own tears before. The following insight is often attributed to St. Óscar Romero: "There are many things that can only be seen through eyes that have cried." To cry is to experience something on a level beyond the intellect, to feel something deep within oneself. When we cry, we not only process and release our own feelings but gain insight into the sorrow of others. Rather than just an intellectual assent to the idea of one's feelings, a mere acknowledgment of another's pain, crying makes it easier to experience another's pain as our own, to approach our neighbor with compassionate empathy.

As our capacity for empathy grows, so, too, does our desire to bring comfort to others. A heart that has been broken seeks to console other broken hearts. It seeks to rectify the situation— to eliminate that which causes sorrow in the first place. For how can it not? When we know what it feels like to have our heart broken, we can no longer walk by another's sorrow and be unaffected. The one who is vulnerable enough to see pain in another and let their heart break—to mourn with those who mourn—cannot go back to their ordinary lives unchanged. They have seen what cannot be unseen, felt what cannot be unfelt, and their heart wants nothing more than to take the sorrowful affliction away from those in pain. This begins with charity, but ultimately leads one to hear the call for justice. The causes of sorrow in our world cannot be tolerated and must be fixed.

When Jesus speaks of the blessedness of those who mourn, this is what he's talking about. This is the true fruit of those who mourn. Jesus is not encouraging us to embrace tragedy or death. Rather, he's asking us to respond to tragedy, pain, and sorrow with vulnerability, compassion, and empathy. When someone's love is so great that it endures through pain, is shared with another, and drives them to build a better world, they are experiencing a taste of the kingdom of heaven in the here and now. Blessed are those who care enough to let their hearts be broken, for they will be comforted.

Turning Outrage into Empathy

When I was in high school, I loved watching late-night comedy shows. In the world immediately after the September 11, 2001, attacks, in a country soon engaged in the War on Terror, there was something therapeutic about hearing comedians give their take on world events, satirizing and mocking the absurdity all around us. I especially liked *The Daily Show with Jon Stewart*, which became the model for so many other shows at the time, for the way that it disarmed the viewer while dealing with serious issues. Stewart's tone was one of ironic detachment as he portrayed a naive observer stumbling through an unreasonable world, shocked by not only the absurdity around him, but by the ease with which everyone accepted it as normal. Through self-deprecating and sarcastic humor, the show reminded us that we are not objective observers outside of or above the issues of society; we are at the center, allowing and even contributing to the absurdity that shocks us. As satire, it was comedy with many layers.

This is in stark contrast to the tone of most late-night shows today. At some point over the last decade, late-night comedians decided to ditch the subtle, naive shtick for an angrier, more direct approach. Outraged by what they are seeing in the world, late-night hosts across the board seem no longer interested in being a part of the joke. Rather, they seem to want to annihilate the absurdity around them. Today, monologues are dominated by vicious insults and overly detailed explainers that mercilessly slice apart the object of the show's anger. Division and despair dominate the viewing experience, providing an outlet for one's unexamined rage to be directed at another. For those who share the host's outrage, these segments can still be as immensely funny as before. They can even be pretty effective at rallying like-minded viewers to a cause.

The shift in comedic tone over the years is hardly accidental. It is but a reflection of the general shift that much of our public discourse has taken. As a people, we do not want to be naive passing observers, shocked and bewildered by the absurdity of our world, happy enough to look the other way. We are a society angry at the way things are. Protests and demonstrations have increased in frequency and reach, attracting what would have normally been fairly apolitical people. Each day the internet seems to implode with rage over a new issue, stuck in an infinite loop of anger, overreaction, and more anger. Election signs and political slogans no longer serve as temporary supports of a candidate or cause during election campaigns, but have become year-round fixtures, a reflection of the overpoliticized and divided nature of our discourse. While politics and religion were never easy to discuss, there is something even more volatile about these topics today—everything and everyone seems supercharged with anger, ready to explode over something.

For some Christians, this approach is justified; it is the necessary tone one must take up in the face of evil. To denounce is biblical. To condemn is the Word of God. To boil over in anger and thrash with all one's fury is what one does when seeing with the eyes of God. Just look at the prophets. From the mouths of holy men come accusations, name-calling, warnings, and condemnations. "Woe to you!" they shout. "Turn from your evil, you obstinate of heart!" To express God's anger, Jeremiah once told the people that they were like rotting underwear to God, good for nothing but to be thrown away. Elijah became so enraged by the idol worship of his time that he challenged the prophets of the false religion to a contest; when they lost, he ordered them all to be executed. These were not polite conversations! And so, some Christians say, we are to do the same, raising our voices and condemning our enemy. It's called "being prophetic."

But is it, really? Is outrage the defining characteristic of a prophet? More important, is condemning another person particularly effective at inspiring change? While it is certainly true that one of the responsibilities of a prophet was to communicate

God's anger with an unfaithful people, it is essential to grasp what that means. God's anger is not our anger. It is not dismissive or petty, seeking pain as its ultimate end, nor does it negate the unbreakable bond that God has with his people. God's anger is always directed toward one thing: reconciliation. It may be harsh at times and spill over in destruction, but it is never permanent. It is never an end in itself. God chastises to bring his people back. He punishes because he wants what's best for his people. He shouts because he is disappointed and heartbroken.

As much as we have been conditioned to read the prophets as angry men filled with outrage, I wonder if we might hear them instead as men so in love with God's people, so set on the vision for God's kingdom, that it breaks their heart when they see things going awry. I wonder if we might hear their words not as having come from them—dejected and downcast human beings at war with their brothers and sisters—but as the voice of God, lamenting the terrible deeds of his people and wanting nothing more than for them to come home. As harsh as the words of the prophets can seem, I can't help but hear sorrow in their voices and longing in their hearts. The reason that they speak at all, risking their lives, is that they care for their nation and refuse to give up. They love even when it would hurt a lot less not to. In other words, they mourn.

There is no doubt that righteous anger has its place in the world. Injustice *should* outrage us; evil *should* cause us to raise our voices. In a later chapter I'll get into how we might go about confronting our enemies firmly and directly, but for now, I would like to suggest that outrage is not our only way to deal with disappointment. In a world of constant outrage, I think we must allow ourselves to be heartbroken from time to time. What if we looked at the things we saw wrong in the world, the people who disappointed us, not as our enemies to be destroyed, but as our fallen-away brothers and sisters suffering tragedies?

What if instead of looking only at the outward conclusion of people's actions, we dug below the surface to feel their pain, to understand why they think and feel the way they do, to cry for the things they cry about? If we allow ourselves to move from outrage to empathy, to feel for those who hurt us, it's possible that we will discover a bruised and broken person, looking for someone to mourn with them.

I remember experiencing this early in my online ministry. Despite being told by many not to "feed the trolls"—that there were people online who just wanted to cause controversy and so should be ignored—I dipped my foot into the water. When someone called me a vile name or posted a derogatory remark about something I stood for, I responded calmly and compassionately, affirming their frustration and asking if there was a way that I could better serve them. I would state in clear but gentle words that what they said was offensive and that they should consider apologizing. Most of my attempts unsurprisingly resulted in more inflammatory comments from the trolls, but not always. Sometimes, the person actually apologized. So disarmed by the fact that another person was treating them with basic respect, they would open up and tell me about the pain they were experiencing, how they were miserable and lost. I can't tell you how many messages I've received from people who once directed their hatred at me, now revealing instead the pain inside of them. Some have been abused by the Church. Some are dealing with unfathomable traumas. Most are just very lonely. It turns out that beneath the harsh, vile exterior of many anonymous accounts are real people, suffering alone, just needing to be heard.

And so it is in the nonvirtual world as well. I'm amazed in the confessional by the burdens some people carry around with them. In so many instances, I have heard the confession of someone I thought I knew—someone I had worked with and enjoyed many conversations with—only to find that they had been quietly suffering for some time. Beneath the surface were feelings of shame and regret, sins that had unsettled them so completely that it took them years to confess them aloud, traumas that had shaken them so deeply that they'd never told another person. On the outside, they may have seemed a little impatient or mean at times, the type of person that might wear on other people's nerves, but after coming to see what plagues them beneath the surface, I'm always struck with awe at how well they have held themselves together, all things considered. I find it impossible to be outraged at them. All I want to do is weep.

In our seminary training, we were encouraged to look beyond the surface of someone's words to get to the heart of who a person is and what they are feeling. A person may lash out at us and say harsh words, but it's possible that they're just displacing the pain of a recent tragedy, guarding their fears, projecting their anger, or feeling altogether lost. Instead of taking it personally and responding with anger ourselves, we were taught that we must learn to cut through their rough exterior to comfort the pain inside. Anger accomplishes little other than producing more anger and too often tears.

Imagine how different our Church and our world would be if we mourned for each other a bit more. When faced with people who seem to us an abomination—standing for everything we stand against, causing harm to those around us, directly attacking God and God's Church—what if we responded with sorrow instead of outrage? What if instead of seeing people as enemies needing to be cast out, we saw them as our brothers and sisters, lost and broken? What if instead of yelling at them, we cried with them?

This is what it means to mourn. To follow Jesus, we need not be the victims of demoralizing tragedies, but we do need to be a people with the capacity to love through sorrow. When the world is in conflict, it seeks to eliminate threats; when the world experiences tragedy, it does everything it can to hide from it. As Christians, we are different. We are a people who love even when it hurts. We know that our shared sorrow only brings us closer together in greater empathy, and we know that a heart that feels is a heart that can heal and reconcile. When we love so freely that we allow ourselves to be heartbroken for others and healed by God, we are on the way of Beatitude.

Questions for Reflection

1. How often do you cry? When was the last time you cried in front of another person? Take some time to reflect on how conscious you are of your own sorrow and how readily you invite others into your feelings.

2. Think about some people in your life that you've struggled to get along with. What sorrows exist in their lives? Are there ways that you can offer comfort to them?

3. Think about the times you've mourned. How have these experiences shaped you? In what ways might you still learn from them?

Practical Acts of Heartbreak

• When you watch the news or read a current-events article about a tragic situation, try to imagine the perspective of the victims. Allow yourself to feel the pain of another, even cry. Don't just intellectualize tragedies and move on. Let yourself feel sorrow.

- When you find yourself in conflict, be conscious of the pain your adversary might be carrying. Look beyond their exterior anger and work to comfort what's hurt beneath.

- In your daily prayer, remember those who suffer tragedies. Keep a list of different types of loss and remember the unknown people who might be struggling all around you.

3. CONFIDENCE

BLESSED ARE THE MEEK

Blessed are the meek, for they will inherit the land.
—Matthew 5:5

Calm the World Cannot Give

When I was in fourth grade, I had a classmate who was as troubled as he was smart. A new student to our school that year, he seemed to struggle to get along with other students, often getting in fights or disassociating completely from others on the playground. Unfortunately, his relationship with the teachers wasn't much better, as he constantly got in trouble for talking back to adults. Rumor had it that his home life was difficult; looking back, I get the sense that he simply didn't know how to handle the fact that he was a genius. All we knew at the time was that he was a volatile kid, and that his explosion one day late in the year was the most incredible, terrifying thing that we had ever seen. Pushed to his breaking point by whatever correction he had just received, he stood up, slammed his desk, and started screaming every swear word he could think of at the teacher. He called her names and insulted her. He used vulgar

29

and derogatory terms that most fourth graders wouldn't even have known, let alone use in front of an adult. He spoke with rage and violence in his voice until he was out of breath.

Needless to say, this was the talk of the school for weeks to come. I don't remember much about that year, but I can hardly imagine that there was anything more jarring and memorable for any student. He was popular for once, albeit for unfortunate reasons.

Interestingly enough, when I think back on that scene today, nearly twenty-five years later, what most sticks out in my mind is not what that student did, but how our teacher responded. Faced with a child having the most epic tantrum imaginable, receiving what was likely the most offensive rebuke of her life, she remained calm. The entire time he screamed at her, she never said a word, never raised her hand, never gave any indication of anger. When he finished, she remained quiet for a few seconds, letting him catch his breath, as she looked at him like she would look at any other student. Then, after what seemed like an eternity to the rest of us, she spoke, ever so calmly and gently: "I'm sorry you feel that way. Is there anything else you would like to say?"

Her words immediately disarmed the boy and restored order to the classroom. While a response as calm as hers may be interpreted by some as passive and weak—cowering beneath the force of an angry adversary—what I witnessed was the exact opposite. This was a woman in complete control. Although it was a direct attack, she did not appear to be the least bit threatened. She didn't lose her temper or become flustered, shouting back at the kid or fleeing in tears. How was she able to do this? She was grounded and confident in who she was. She had been yelled at, yes, but by a fourth grader. She was being insulted, yes, but by someone who didn't actually know her enough to hurt her in a way that mattered. The reason the teacher responded with patience, understanding, and a general sense of peace was not that she couldn't stand up to an angry fourth grader. It was that she didn't *have* to. Aware of the fact that neither her sense of worth nor her personal security was legitimately threatened, she had an inner calm that this little boy could not shake. This was a profound example to our class of what it means to be meek.

Too often in our daily language the word "meek" is used as a synonym for "weak." When we think of someone who is meek, we imagine a demure old lady, a passive little boy—someone peaceful, but peaceful because they have no other choice: they're cowardly, incapable, or entirely afraid. The world is a big, scary place, and so the "meek" have chosen to hide from it, staying out of its way lest they get hurt.

The reality is that there is nothing weak or cowardly about being meek. Quite the opposite, actually. What makes someone meek is not fear, but rather unflappable courage. The meek person remains quiet because they feel no need to speak; they respond with peace because there is nothing to threaten them. When I think of the word "meek," what comes to mind are the old, wise martial arts masters often depicted in Hollywood movies. No matter the situation, they sit calmly. Large, foreboding attackers may approach, but they remain at peace. They are neither alarmed nor triggered, they neither speak nor attack, because they don't need to. Even if the attacker is unaware of the power of the master (although never for too long!), the master is so confident in his skills that there is no reason to become flustered. The master's calm appearance reflects the fact that he has tamed his power in such a way that he has courage not to use it.

This is what Jesus possesses and models to the disciples. Here was a man who rarely raised his voice and never threw a punch, who offered no resistance when he was arrested and subsequently executed, and yet possessed more power than any man could. Beneath his peaceful exterior was confidence that no one could shake, trust that not even the devil could break. He was not going to be provoked, but he never cowered. He knew what was true and what wasn't, and there was no need to lose control over it.

The meekness that Jesus possessed in his earthly life did not come so much from *who*, but rather *whose*, he was. He knew that he was the Son of the Father. How many times did he say that he was going to the Father because he came from the Father? How many times did he teach that he and the Father are one? Throughout his ministry, in word and in deed, Jesus made it abundantly clear that he knew where he came from, who he was, and where he was going. There was no identity crisis, nor was there ever a sense of hesitancy in his actions. He acted with confidence—teaching, preaching, healing, admonishing, and even remaining silent, at times—because he knew that he did not belong to this world but existed before it began. He was grounded in the relationship he shared with the Father in heaven.

Because of this, he could live with docility before the Father, trusting in his every word with patience. With unflappable confidence in his identity, he was not tempted to give in to anxiety or distress, and had no impulse to go ahead on his own. The Father was in control, and that was enough for him. It's no wonder, then, that Psalm 37—the psalm on which this Beatitude is based—teaches that "those who wait for the LORD will inherit the earth" (v. 9). Jesus was meek because he patiently waited on the Father. He sat in prayer listening. Despite his agony in the garden, despite his own desire that the cup should pass him by, his confidence in the Father was so strong that he met the Father with an open mind and heart, living as he taught us to pray, "thy will be done." Things may have seemed bleak in the moment, but his unwavering confidence kept him steadfast and patient.

It is from this profound sense of patience that Jesus ultimately responded to the world as he did, returning violence and ridicule with peace. When we think of what he went through, it is almost too much to bear. He performed miracles and was called a liar; he taught the truth and was called a blasphemer; he included the sinner and outcast and was himself excluded as a sinner; he offered life to the world and the world took his own. On almost every page of each of the gospels, Jesus is faced with criticism and hate, and yet he resisted retaliation. Through it all, he endured injury without resentment, holding his tongue even through his Passion.

To the casual observer, this may appear to be a sign of weakness, that Jesus was afraid or unable. To the Christian, it is a profound witness of his meekness. Knowing his place in the Father, trusting in his Father's providential care, Jesus lived and died knowing that all he wanted was to be with the Father and that there was nothing the world could ever do to prevent that from happening. As the saying goes, "Sticks and stones may break my bones, but words will never break me." Grounded in who he was, there was nothing that could upset his inmost calm to the point of violence. Jesus was not weak. He simply had control over his power.

This is precisely what Jesus is looking for in his disciples. Not morally weak pushovers who will cower under pressure! Not people that hide in the back because they're afraid of their own shadows! He wants people who are so confident in who they are and where they're going that nothing in the world can cause them to lose control. In the case of his disciples, this confidence does not come from themselves but from their faith in God. Where they're going is not of their choosing—they may not even know it themselves—but their trust in God is so strong that there is no need to worry. As with Jesus in his own life, they are so rooted in a relationship with the Father that nothing can ever unsettle them, not even the Cross. They accept it willingly, without fear or doubt, because they live with the power of God in them. The meek know that nothing can ever really harm them, and so they sit calmly like a martial arts master, walk confidently with their divine teacher, trusting in the providential care of the Father.

In this way, Jesus not only says that the meek will inherit the land in a future, end-times reality, but that they are already blessed in the very act of being meek. Living in this way is its own reward. For unlike the poor and those who mourn—people who are blessed because they find hope and meaning through their suffering—the meek are so grounded in the grace of God that the suffering of this world no longer threatens or scares them. They live with such confidence in God that, like St. Paul writing to the Corinthians, they can look at death and ask, "Where . . . is your sting?" (1 Cor 15:55). When the meek look at the divisions and despair of the world, all that comes to mind is the fact that nothing can separate them from the love of God—not "anguish, or distress, or persecution, or famine, or nakedness, or peril, or the sword" (Rom 8:35). Innermost calm like that is its own reward. It is enduring peace that the world can neither give nor take away.

When Jesus speaks of the blessedness of the meek, this is what he's talking about. Those who give their entire trust to God, courageously follow even when they don't know the way, and endure insult with peace and confidence, truly embody the life, death, and resurrection of Jesus Christ. Put another way, they live a blessed life. Some may interpret their outward demeanor as weakness or passivity, but what they possess is strength unrivaled in our world. Even here and now, they are experiencing a taste of the kingdom of heaven. Blessed are those who have confidence in the Lord, for they will inherit the land.

Easing Our Triggers

I have a friend who is a bit of a sports fanatic. He doesn't just casually watch his team; he lives, breathes, and routinely loses his mind over everything they do. Most of the time his ridiculous reactions are amusing to the rest of us, and so we play to his triggers just to get a rise out of him. A simple question about last season, the mention of a particular player's name, even an offhand comment about the rival team's city can launch him into a rant that even he has no control over, with the result that we sit and watch, wondering how long it will take for him to realize we're messing with him. (What are friends for but to have a little fun with, right?) If only it always remained playful. The problem with some superfans like my friend is that they are never really joking and never really in control. Certain things, no matter their context or intent, can set them off and ruin a moment. Sometimes a single word can alter their mood. Although funny at times, their passion can leave everyone else tiptoeing through sentences and avoiding certain topics lest we stumble into an argument. This can be a bit tiring.

Unfortunately, situations like these are not exclusive to super sports fans, nor are they all that rare in our society today. We live in an anxious world. Everywhere I look, I see people highly passionate about a particular issue, lifestyle, or belief system, while at the same time extremely sensitive and easily triggered. The mere mention of someone's name can be enough to set some people off and derail a conversation. Around certain people, we know to avoid particular topics because there's a good chance of a hostile response. For so many people—probably all of us, from time to time—it takes very little to go from being sensible and rational to feeling tense and ready to fight.

It's amazing to watch it happen in my own life. I'll be having a normal conversation with someone, amicably talking about this or that, and it will just happen. Someone will say something that I know is patently untrue. Maybe it's a common misconception or political talking point we hear all the time, maybe it's an outright conspiracy theory. I can't explain it and I wish I could control it, but something clicks within me that leaves me immediately unsettled. Regardless of the context or intent of the speaker, something about hearing statements that I know to be untrue elevates my pulse, tenses my muscles, furrows my brow, and unfortunately, sharpens my words. I remember this happening once at a parishioner's house while I was a seminarian. A family had invited the friars to dinner and been excellent hosts . . . until one of them started talking about scientific "research" she had found, and why it was immoral for Catholics to have their children vaccinated. I would like to think I bit my tongue for at least long enough for her to finish her sentence, but I know I didn't. Something bubbled up inside of me that had to be spoken immediately. Manners didn't matter. Different perspectives didn't matter. I couldn't let such blatantly wrong information slide uncorrected, and so I corrected it. We were not invited back.

How easy it is to catastrophize a situation and lose sight of what matters. *Lies are being spoken. Truth is at stake!* How easy it is to go from a nice, amicable conversation to forcefully correcting another person. *No, actually, that's wrong!* Without even realizing it, many of us have an impulse to jump in and correct people. For me, the problem in this situation wasn't that I cared for the truth or even that I attempted to correct the host of the house. It's that my response was driven by emotion, and almost entirely involuntary. There is a trigger in me that can set off without warning.

Outbursts of emotion like these—from the rabid superfan, the obnoxious political activist, the relentless know-it-all—all share something in common: they arise from something within us that feels threatened. Unlike my fourth-grade teacher who remained calm and peaceful because she knew a child could not hurt her and that in fact the child was acting out of his own deep hurt, we reveal something within us in these kinds of situations that actually fears being harmed. The insecurities that lie beneath the surface come to light and grab hold of our emotions. Conscious of them or not, we find ourselves unsettled and defensive in their presence, ready to pounce, because we no longer feel in control. Our power is not enough to protect us and the things we love.

When this happens, defensiveness becomes our dominant disposition. I remember working with someone once who was constantly criticizing everything and everyone around him. If he didn't like something about you, he let you know. Besides being unbearable to be around under normal circumstances, this person happened to be my direct supervisor at the time. Whether true or not, I perceived him as a threat to my well-being, someone who could cause me harm. Whenever I was around him, I tensed up, anticipating his criticisms, ready to pounce if he said anything critical. On more than a few occasions I snapped back with quick retorts, putting him in his place.

At first, my behavior seemed entirely justified to me. My words were the direct result of this man's constant criticism: he represented an actual, serious threat to my well-being, and so he deserved my outbursts. There were definitely times when it was right and necessary to stand up to him, even if I did so in a harsh manner.

The problem was that he wasn't always being critical. In fact, most of the time he was quite nice, simply unaware of the way people perceived him. In many cases, it would seem, the frustration I felt wasn't linked so much to things he actually did as to my own defensive attitude. Because of how I felt about him in general, I entered every encounter on edge, feeling threatened and ready to attack. My hypersensitivity to the mere possibility of a threat caused me to see danger when it did not really exist, and unfortunately, this meant that there were plenty of times that I attacked unnecessarily. I lashed out with a sarcastic remark, passive-aggressive action, or flustered, defensive resistance to what I was being asked to do. I regrettably let my emotions get the best of me, dictating not only how I treated him, but how I perceived all situations involving him.

But here's what's crazy about it all, as I look back on it now: there was never really a threat at all. Sure, he was my direct supervisor, but there was no chance that he was going to fire me. In fact, there really wasn't *anything* he could have done to actually hurt me. He could criticize and belittle, but so what? At the end of the day, if I really thought about it, I didn't care what he thought of me. My life wasn't the slightest bit better or worse based on his opinion. And yet I treated him like a threat. I let him get under my skin and control my emotions.

I don't think it's said enough today, but we have much more control over how we feel and, perhaps more important, how we respond to our feelings, than we often acknowledge. People can treat us in ways that are mean, disrespectful, arrogant, offensive, or downright disgusting, and this may hurt us deeply, but we are not without agency to address the pain and anger that well up within us. We can be persecuted, yelled at, harassed, spat upon, or even assaulted, but for most of us (we who are free from serious, often debilitating mental illness), there is no intrinsic reason that we *must* feel angry and even less reason to accept that we need to keep feeling angry. Instead of flying off into a rage, we can see such situations as an opportunity for penance and so rejoice; we can choose to focus on the waywardness of our attackers and so weep for them and pray for their release; we can choose to focus instead on positive aspects of the world and smile in gratitude for all of the gifts we've received. We can, and really must, take control of our emotional lives. Some may know how to push our buttons better than others, and we know of course that abusive relationships, trauma, and mental illness leave many without full control of their emotions, but we must always remind ourselves that we have agency in the matter. However limited, we still have choices about how to respond to our difficult emotions.

Again I say, "Sticks and stones may break my bones, but words will never break me." This is precisely the definition of what it means to be meek. When we possess such self-control of our emotions that we can be triggered to anger or rage by no one, instead living with patience and confidence—we are blessed.

In the end, this is only possible in the Lord. This is only possible if we Christians remember *whose* we are, trusting completely in the providential care of the Father, and so live with the confidence that there is ultimately nothing that can keep us from the satisfaction of the kingdom of heaven. *Nothing.* We read St. Paul's famous words to the Romans (8:35–39) on a regular basis, but I'm not sure we ever really let them change our hearts. Imagine if we actually believed what he said. Imagine if we began every day, entered every conversation, started every prayer, and ended every argument with the words "nothing can separate us from the love of God." Imagine how different our world would be . . . how different our dispositions would be toward the things that bother us.

To follow Jesus, we need not cower before the enemies of God or become passive doormats before our adversaries, but we do need to be people who trust in God's providence. The kingdom of heaven may not come quickly and we may have to endure our own passion along the way, but there is nothing but blessedness for those who trust in the Lord. When we are able to trust with confidence, knowing that we could return violence with violence but that there isn't the slightest need to do so, we are on the way of Beatitude.

Questions for Reflection

1. Where do you find confidence in life? What makes you feel calm and in control? Is this something that is steadfast and reliable, or does it come and go in you?

2. Are you a patient person? How do you act when you have to wait on someone or something? Take a few moments thinking about why that is. Is this something you want to change? How can you do so?

3. What things cause you to lose your temper? Do you find that people can easily get a rise out of you? How do you regain composure when this happens?

Practical Acts of Confidence

*   Spend time in prayer remembering the many ways that God is more in control of the world than you are. Think about the immensity of God's power and how infinitesimally small we are. Rather than give you anxiety, let these thoughts remind you of God's infinite providence that protects us and leads us to good things.

*   When someone does something that annoys you or challenges your sensibilities, ask yourself, *Does it really matter?* If it doesn't, allow yourself to remain quiet and move on.

*   Before getting out of bed each morning, say to yourself, *Nothing can separate us from the love of God.* Repeat this three times slowly. Then, before going to bed at the end of your day, ask yourself, *Did anything separate me from the love of*

God today? If something did, give it to God in prayer and commit to doing better the next day.

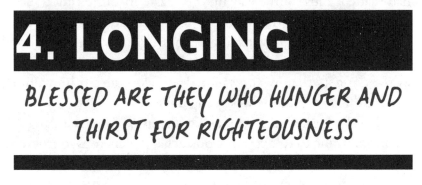

4. LONGING

BLESSED ARE THEY WHO HUNGER AND THIRST FOR RIGHTEOUSNESS

> Blessed are they who hunger and thirst for righteousness, for they will be satisfied.
>
> —Matthew 5:6

Driven by Desperation

I once met a man at a refugee camp in Mexico who was attempting to cross the southern border of the United States. He was from one of the Central American countries, meaning that he had already traveled a few hundred miles to get to where he was, and that he still had more than a thousand miles to go before he arrived at the border. He was hoping to hitch a ride on the back of the train that ran through town but knew it was a dangerous way to travel—not only did the police monitor the railways but also traffickers and gang members were always looking for people to extort. The center itself was founded some years earlier after seventy-two such migrants were killed attempting to make it to the United States. I couldn't help but look with dread at what he was likely going to face in the coming days, and did my part to warn him of what could happen.

But he knew it all already. This was not his first harrowing journey up the Mexican coast to the American border. Twice he had made it most of the way up the coast, encountering police and traffickers, and bribing people just enough to stay alive, only to come up short. Now, having been caught and deported for the third time, he was beginning the journey again, fully aware of the dangers that awaited him. He wasn't sure if he would survive this time, but he was going anyway.

Naively, I asked him why he kept trying, given the danger. "Why continue to risk your life on such a treacherous journey?" Matter-of-factly, he responded, "How can I not? My whole *life* is there." As it turns out, he was once successful on his trip across the border, fifteen years ago. On his own, he managed to get all the way from Central America to Texas and set up a home there. He found a job, bought a house, paid taxes, and eventually met a woman and fell in love with her. She was a fellow immigrant from his country of origin. After a few years, the two of them married, had two daughters, and settled into a normal life in their new country. When he said that his whole life was in the United States, he wasn't kidding. "What choice do I have? Even if it might kill me, I have to try."

In our world, there are countless people with stories just like this man, desperately fighting to stay alive. I think of the communities torn apart by gun violence, whose residents live in fear and stay locked up at all times. I was once assigned to a church in an area of the country where the violence was so prevalent that when I arrived, the pastor took me around on what the staff referred to as the "murder tour" of the city. "Two people were shot on that corner last month . . . a parishioner was mugged and killed in that store right there, very sad funeral . . . a lot of gang violence happens on that street." The lives of those in the city were defined by it. They longed for something different. From a position of desperation—literally, their lives depended on change—they organized task forces, demanded meetings with city councilors, and peacefully demonstrated in the streets. If you asked them why they did it, they would answer, "How can we not?"

Maybe the most apparent example of desperation in our world today can be heard in the voices of those fighting for racial equality. I recently listened as an elderly black man shared with anguish the struggles of his life. His father had been a sharecropper, his grandfather a slave. For eighty years he had been discriminated against, rejected, and forced to live as a second-class citizen. All he could do was fight back tears as he pondered aloud, "When will this nonsense end? Will we ever get it right?" This is the attitude that so many people bring to the streets these days; this is the longing that defines the lives of so many people of color. They protest because they can't go on any longer with things as they are. Something has to change or they won't survive. They fight on because they have no other choice. "How can we not?"

In each of these situations, what seems to define people who keep fighting is a sense of urgency: they refuse to accept the present world as it is. Everything they do is motivated by an immense and immediate longing for something greater—the knowledge that what they are doing is a matter of life and death. Nothing else is as important as this. Everything else deserves less attention. For what choice do they have? To give in for a day, to ease up their vigilance, would seal their fate and forfeit that which they desire most.

For many of us, the closest we can come to understanding this sense of urgency is the experience of our physiological needs: hunger and thirst. Everyone knows how different the world seems when you're hungry, even if for just a few hours. I think of the time that I forgot to eat breakfast before my elementary-school class trip to Washington, DC. For weeks, this trip was all I could think about—the giant elephant in the National Museum of Natural History, the lunar module in the National Air and Space Museum, the grandeur of the Capitol building. I imagined it to be a day that I would always remember. Then hunger set in. Today, all I recall is how painfully hungry I was all morning, how my only thought for hours was when I would be able to eat. I honestly don't even remember if we made it to any of the places I wanted to visit. At this point, all I can picture is the food court where I finally had a meal. How powerful a grip our physiological needs can have on us! When we are hungry, nothing else matters.

This is the image that Jesus chooses to use for the fourth Beatitude. In Luke's gospel, the image is a literal one—physical hunger and thirst—whereas Matthew's gospel points to a people with more spiritual ambitions—hunger and thirst *for righteousness*. In either case, whether literal or metaphorical, the people Jesus is addressing are not those who are temporarily inconvenienced by hunger, who simply need a snack, who know that what satisfies is right around the corner. No, he speaks to a desperate people—those who suffer from starvation and dehydration, who struggle to survive under the tyranny of injustice. Unless they are satisfied soon, they will perish.

As with the other Beatitudes, Jesus appears at first to glorify an overwhelmingly uncomfortable experience as a sign of blessedness, but once again, his focus is not the affliction itself. In both gospels, the essence of what makes people blessed is their sense of urgency. Whether it is a literal or spiritual hunger, what makes someone fit for the kingdom, now and in the future, is not the immediate affliction that they endure but the spiritual fruit that it can produce. Those who hunger and thirst know that it is not enough to sit back and wait for their needs to be met. They cannot afford to take no for an answer. If they are going to survive, they must take action, and they must do it with all their energy.

Too often in our spiritual lives we equate trusting in the Lord with a passive approach to life. We kneel before God with our prayers and then wait for God to answer them, doing nothing ourselves. This is a deficient approach to prayer. While it is essential to trust wholly in God's providence and never act outside of God's will (see chapter 3), it is also crucial to remember that God's providence *includes* our actions. The God we believe in is not a figure like Santa Claus, hearing requests from afar and impersonally granting gifts. Our God is an incarnational God, one who lives in and through every aspect of our existence. The Father sent his Son to live in the world as a part of the world for the sake of the world. The Holy Spirit was breathed into the disciples and so guides the Church's actions from within. As disciples of Christ, we show our obedience to God not in sitting idly by, waiting for him to act for us; we show our obedience by acting as Jesus has taught, taking up his mission where he left off, remembering that his final words before the Ascension were, "And behold, I am with you always, until the end of the age" (Mt 28:20). Jesus does not want people to pray to God and then go about their lives with indifference, waiting passively on the Lord; he wants people with such hunger and thirst for the kingdom of heaven that it is really all they care about.

For, what does it say about a disciple if they are able to look at the world as it is and remain unaffected? What does it say about a person if they are able to offer their prayers without desperation for change? To go to God in prayer for things that do not satisfy, to ask for things that are not essential to our salvation, is a privilege that only the comfortable are afforded. The truly hungry do not pray because they are slightly inconvenienced or wish for some luxury in their lives—they pray

because they know their lives depend on it. They pray because
the world is a far cry from what it needs to be. Like Peter after
Jesus offered the bread of life, they say, "Master, to whom shall
we go? You have the words of eternal life" (Jn 6:68). Like the
woman at the well, recognizing Jesus as the one who will truly
satisfy, they say, "Sir, give me this water, so that I may not be
thirsty or have to keep coming here to draw water" (Jn 4:15).
For how can they not?

Throughout our history, holy men and women have burned
with desire for the kingdom of heaven. They have lived with a
hunger so great that everything else fades away. I think of the
holy longing of St. Monica, a mother who agonized over the
waywardness of her son Augustine and prayed without ceasing
that he would accept the faith of Christianity. I'm moved by the
immense passion with which St. Francis of Assisi lived, so desperate to be with God that he imitated the life of Jesus in all that
he did, ultimately being gifted with the stigmata. I'm inspired
by the sense of urgency of Servant of God Dorothy Day, a jour-
nalist and political activist so unsettled by the vast exploitation
of the poor and the violence in the world that she took her faith
to the streets, founding the Catholic Worker Movement and
actively fighting for justice into her late seventies.

When Jesus speaks of the blessedness of those who hunger
and thirst, this is what he's talking about. The ones who hunger
and thirst will be satisfied, not just in a future reality but in
the here and now, precisely because they do not take no for an
answer. They seek what is good and do not give up. Commit-
ting every aspect of their lives with a single-minded devotion
to the source of life itself, they not only long with great passion
for the future coming of the kingdom of heaven, but are intent
on doing their part to hasten its coming *today*. The hungry do
not simply await satisfaction but receive the bread of life and
fountain of salvation already in their midst. It is by this alone

that they are able to persevere, nourished by the foretaste of the future banquet. Blessed are those who long with great desire for the kingdom of heaven, for they will be satisfied.

Rekindling Desire

Believe it or not, there was a time before the internet and smartphones when kids were not glued to their screens but played outside and made their own fun. I believe, as a child of the '90s, I was the last generation of kids to know what this was like. Our house didn't have internet until I was in middle school; there were no cell phones in our house until I was sixteen (and even then, there was barely anything to do with them but make phone calls!). If we wanted to have fun, we searched the neighborhood for friends and made it ourselves. It's amazing, looking back now, to think how freely we roamed the neighborhood on our bikes; as long as we were home by a certain time, we never had to tell my parents where we were going or what we planned to do. It was a liberating experience as an eleven-year-old. That is, if you had a bike worthy of riding.

My siblings and I always had bikes, but they were never the cool ones. More often than not, our bikes were hand-me-downs from our neighbors or cousins, meaning that the first bike I rode without training wheels was aqua colored and had flowers printed on it. It was an old bike from the girl next door. Hardly the sort of thing that an eleven-year-old boy could ride around the neighborhood with his friends! I desperately wanted a new bike.

As it turns out, bikes are expensive, and my parents were a little too busy paying a mortgage and putting food on the table to go right out and buy me one. But this was not an option. I *needed* a new bike. I started saving my allowance each week, forgoing the immediate gratification of candy or baseball cards for a future desire, in the hopes of buying one myself. Almost immediately, I realized that my wages were far below any labor standards acceptable in the developed world and that it would take me years to collect enough money at that pace. Turning to plan B, I convinced my parents to let me get a paper route in my neighborhood. And then another one right next to it. I saved everything I made for weeks and weeks, dreaming about what it would be like to have a cool bike. I went to the bike shop a few times to look at my options and eventually decided that it wasn't enough just to have a *cool* bike; I wanted the *coolest* bike. That, of course, meant saving a bit more, waiting a little while longer. I worked and saved and rode around on an uncool bike, motivated by my desire to have something that I *really* wanted. Eventually purchasing that bike was the most satisfying thing my eleven-year-old self could even imagine.

When we look at the waywardness of the world, it can be easy to conclude that our society is suffering from an excess of desire. We want too much. We're too materialistic. Many will say that our childhood desire for toys has gotten out of hand. Lavish lifestyles are portrayed as the ideal form of life; sexual promiscuity is accepted as the norm; food and drink are consumed at every opportunity in any quantity. If we're looking for the cause of our sinful attitudes in the world, it's hard not to point to avarice, lust, and gluttony, distortions of desire. *Take what you want, when you want, how you want.* The pursuit of one's desires is the anthem of a generation.

I'm not so sure. While there's no doubt that avarice, lust, and gluttony are problems in our world, I can't help but think that the real underlying issue at play here isn't a *distortion* of desire, but complete and utter *loss* of desire. As strange as it may sound, I would like to suggest that the excesses of sensuality that we witness in the world are not the result of overflowing passions too great to be controlled, but desires so weak and disparate that most people no longer even know what they want and so decide to consume whatever is readily available at the moment. What we're witnessing is not a world driven by distorted passions but a world that foolishly accepts immediate gratification rather than examining its true desires.

This is due, in part, to the way in which the world works these days. In a globalized society where travel is quick and commerce is efficient, the distinction of place is fading away. Most cities of a certain size in this country provide expected services, offer a variety of foods, feature many of the same retail stores, and have similar subcultures. Whether something is in season or out of season, it can likely be found at a local store or restaurant—or if not, it can certainly be found online. So much is now available within minutes, in many cases without even leaving one's home. Whereas people before had to travel great distances for what they wanted or wait a long time for something to arrive—like getting a paper route and saving money for months!—there is no longer any need to wait for anything. Gratification is almost simultaneous with impulse.

In a world characterized by immediate gratification, there is rarely enough opportunity for one's desires to actually become manifest. There is no longing that develops in one's heart, no overwhelming hunger that demands attention. The ease with which we can access nearly *everything* diminishes our desire for *anything* in particular. Why would we drive an hour for something we really want when we can get something almost as good ten minutes away? Why wait for two months for the best thing when the sufficient thing is available now? When nearly everything is accessible and nothing requires sacrifice, we eventually find ourselves slipping into a strange state in which we have neither urgency nor patience. There is nothing that compels us more than anything else. We may give in to our impulses and make avaricious, lustful, or gluttonous choices, but our sins are not wholly those of desire. True desire has failed to even develop, leaving us with something far worse than distorted desires—a weakened ability to choose what is truly good because we have ceased caring about the good. All we want is the convenient.

Spiritually speaking, this state of being has a name: acedia. Often associated with the word "sloth" and thus treated as synonymous with "laziness," acedia is far more than a physical condition of inactivity. From the Greek *akēdia,* it literally means "without care." Those who struggle with this sin may appear lazy—idly sitting by, listlessly going about life, refusing to work—but they may also act in a frenetic way, filling their lives with fruitless activity in order to avoid the weightier demands of a healthy spiritual life. Serious decisions are put aside for the sake of menial tasks, diligent planning traded for a path of least resistance. Nothing is inspiring enough to motivate because nothing matters for the spiritually apathetic.

Continuing with the analogy of hunger, we might say that acedia is similar to the habit of constantly snacking. When we fill ourselves with cheap, readily available food whenever we feel a twinge of hunger, we eventually forget what it's like to be really hungry and may never become entirely full. Ever placing whatever is before us in our mouths, we do not experience the aching hunger that drives us to true nourishment, nor the complete satisfaction of a full, hard-earned meal. Had my parents gone right out and bought me a cheap and moderately cool bike, had I purchased the first one that I was able to afford, I suspect there would have been less of a sense of satisfaction. I can guarantee you that I would not have cherished the bike as I did or taken care of it with such diligence. Things that come easily and frequently, without sacrifice or a deep sense of yearning, often fail to mean much to us.

In a world of divisiveness and despair, acedia runs rampant as a safe escape. For many, it does not begin with a cold, apathetic heart, but with the growing fear that our actions aren't making any difference in the world. I've seen it happen to people who were once fanatical advocates for justice. Inspired by the Gospel, they start off with a strong passion for an issue, ready to change the world. *Jesus will bring about justice in our world! The Holy Spirit will renew the face of the earth!* I remember feeling this way about ecological justice, believing that the future was in our hands. We had the ability to recycle, to choose cleaner fuels, to live in a way that treated the earth as the gift of creation that it is rather than a mass to be exploited.

But then impatience crept in. Failures began to mount. I worked to make a difference, and no difference appeared to come. I saw apathetic people who couldn't be bothered to get involved with what I thought was important, and I saw far more powerful forces than me working to undermine the little progress I accomplished. The world needed a large-scale revolution, and I couldn't even get the friars around me to start recycling! Eventually, the task no longer seemed as manageable as it did before, and the hunger that once drove my efforts got filled by other things. As new issues arose, the temptation was to retreat more and more.

This is the great danger of acedia. Rather than a sin of desire, it is a sin that diminishes desire and deadens the conscience. The spiritual apathetic no longer believes that there is anything worth fighting for, no longer lives with desperation for change, no longer yearns for God's intercession. When the condition is devastating enough, the once passionate person chooses not to take a stand or get involved in anything. Rather than set himself up for greater disappointment, he steps back, convincing himself that he doesn't care anymore. The person without desire begins to accept the world as it is—imperfect and broken— believing that she can do nothing that will bring about change. Eventually, for fear of recognizing evil—or God forbid, realizing that he might be the *cause* of such evil!—the apathetic person accepts the false notion that there is nothing inherently better or worse than anything else in the world. Each thing just *is*.

Thus, they give in to avarice, lust, or gluttony—not because they deeply desire it, but because there's nothing left to care about. Consuming whatever snack requires the least resistance, they do not experience enough hunger to drive them to search for nourishment, nor are they ever fully satisfied. How sad it is see someone in this state! You would almost rather they be passionately sinning, chasing after distorted desires, for at least they would desire *something*! At least they would live for *something*! Instead, we see an overabundance of impulsiveness.

As Christians struggling with the division and despair of our world, we must find a way to rekindle true desire in those around us. We must remind people that there is reason to hope, that the kingdom of heaven is inbreaking in our midst. For all that is wrong with the world, the pain and suffering, there are also tremendous signs of the work of God renewing the face of the earth all around us. Look at the tremendous progress the people of God have made fighting for racial equality all around the world! Look at the incredible advancements in medicine and the heroic works of sacrifice on display in hospitals every day! Look at the way millions of people, in every country on earth, love one another, stand up for what's right and just, show mercy to complete strangers, and refuse to give up even when the world is stacked against them! I tell you, the Holy Spirit is present in our midst for all to see. God is inspiring minds with wisdom and knowledge, enflaming hearts with courage and understanding.

Sometimes we just need to look with the eyes of faith and seek with a hungry heart. Despite tremendous challenges, many people persevere. They overcome. They forge on in their desire for righteousness in our world because they have tasted it and know that they will never be satisfied by anything else. It is this immense hunger that drives them, and their unwillingness to sacrifice that is a great sign of the kingdom of heaven already taking hold in this world.

This is what it means to hunger and thirst for righteousness. To be a disciple of Christ, we need not die of starvation or dehydration, but we must know what it feels like to be desperate. Much of our world has grown satisfied with the way things are and so knows nothing of desire. It knows little of hope, sacrifice, perseverance, and urgency. As Christians, we are called to sit in the discomfort of our present age, to let the dissatisfaction of the way things are drive us to want something more. We mustn't hide from it, and we mustn't grow weary. Let the yearning in our hearts grow so painful that we cannot bear the thought of living another day in this way, and let that sense of urgency, guided by the light of faith, pour over into the life of the world. When we refuse to accept anything less than the kingdom of heaven, we are on the way of Beatitude.

Questions for Reflection

1. Recall a time when you desperately wanted something. Think back to how you felt about that desire. If you ended up obtaining it, how did it feel when your desire was fulfilled? If you never received what you so deeply wanted, what happened to your desire?

2. How hard do you work to achieve what you want? Do you give up if things don't come easily, or do you work harder?

3. When you look at the world with a Christian heart, do you burn with a sense of urgency or are you okay with the way things are? Take a moment to think about what motivates you and what you desire deep down. After reading this chapter, are you content with your desires and motivations? Do they conform to the Gospel?

Practical Acts of Longing

- The next time you're thinking about making a significant purchase, give yourself a waiting period before you actually buy. Try attaching certain conditions to the purchase, such as, "I have to go to the gym six times before I buy this" or "I have to do ten acts of kindness first."

- Go out of your way to get what you truly desire, not just what's most convenient. Every once in a while, allow yourself the time and energy to do something that is wildly inconvenient just so that you get in the habit of making sacrifices for important things.

- Look for people in your area who have to work night and day just to survive. Notice the desperation that they live with and take one purposeful action to relieve the longing for basic resources that they are forced to live with each day.

5. SOLIDARITY

BLESSED ARE THE MERCIFUL

> Blessed are the merciful, for they will be shown mercy.
> —Matthew 5:7

Undeserved Abundance

One of the things I've come to treasure most as an adult is the fact that I still keep in touch with a dozen or so of my friends from college. Even after I joined the friars, even as we've all moved away from one another, we've maintained the friendships we started nearly fifteen years ago during our freshman year. It's a thrill for me to get to see them each winter, joining together in the mountains where we rent a house for a weekend. I often go 362 days without seeing any of them, but then we pick up right where we left off—laughing, reminiscing, and enjoying each other's company. Friends like these are not easy to find, and events like this are not something I ever want to miss.

Unfortunately, that is not something always within my control. As someone who's taken a vow of *poverty*, I can't easily pull off traveling across the country to spend a weekend in a gorgeous mountain house. In addition to the limited time I have for vacation, it's just expensive. Each year I try to plan ahead, saving a bit of my stipend each month to cover the trip, but it doesn't always work out. One year, I resigned myself to the fact that I wouldn't be able to make it. It was going to come down to a choice of either visiting my parents for Christmas or hanging out with my friends for New Year's, and we all know how that was going to end. I hinted to one of my friends that it might be difficult that year, trying to sneak out without causing much trouble. But that wasn't going to do. A few days later, another friend sent me a message saying that my absence was unacceptable and that the group had decided to split my costs so I could make it. Because of my awesome friends, I have *never* missed a New Year's get-together. There is a sense of solidarity that binds us together, always reminding us that we are in this together.

When I think about where this comes from, I realize that I haven't done anything to earn this gift, and my friends certainly don't owe me anything. Their commitment to me led them to an act of self-sacrifice, an act of inconvenience that served them in no direct way. How easy it would have been for them to complain! How understandable it would have been for them to say it's not fair that I get something for free while they have to pay extra! But they didn't. What my friends showed me that year is why we remain friends to this day: mercy.

For many people, the idea of mercy is a difficult one to grasp. From the perspective of the one giving mercy, it makes little to no objective sense. Why would someone take what is rightfully theirs and give it to someone who neither deserves it nor can in any way pay it back? What benefit do they gain? In the case of my friends, the need for repayment might be easy to overlook, given the relatively small sum of money, but the concept is no different from creditors seeking payment for past-due bills or the state seeking the death penalty for a murder conviction. Our culture tends to support the idea that when something has been taken that was not earned or deserved, something is owed in its place. Many people believe that to forgo an effort to restore what was unfairly gained is to forgo *justice*, and this simply cannot stand. Society crumbles without justice.

And yet, this is precisely how God operates. While many have an image of God in the Old Testament as full of wrath and out for retribution (and there are certainly some instances in which this is the case), most of the time God is defined by abundant mercy. When Joseph was imprisoned in Egypt, God made "the chief jailer well-disposed toward him" (Gn 39:21). When the Israelites found themselves enslaved in Egypt, God heard their cry and led them to the Promised Land. Most famously, Psalm 136 repeats the chorus "for his mercy endures forever" in each of its twenty-six verses. While it is true that God's anger flared up against the people at one point and their kingdom was destroyed, it's important to remember that this was only after four hundred years of prophets warning the people of their false worship and injustice. Fifteen of Israel's kings are described in the Old Testament as doing evil in the sight of the Lord. After all of that, God's wrath was followed almost immediately by healing and restoration. That is a lot more patience and mercy than is often credited to God in the Old Testament, but it's true! It's why the Old Testament mentions multiple times that God punishes the wicked to the third or fourth generation but has mercy down to the thousandth generation for those who love him. On nearly every page, he shows himself to be a God that hears the cries of the downtrodden, frees the oppressed, forgives the sinner, defends the widow and orphan, *and has patience when his people repeatedly break the covenant.* Time and again, God shows mercy, giving blessing to those who do not deserve it and cannot repay it.

To understand why God acts with mercy, it's helpful to consider the Hebrew word most used to describe God: *hesed.* While most often translated into English as "mercy" or "kindness," the word suggests something far greater than a mere outward show of niceties. Imbedded in the word is a sense of steadfast fidelity and overwhelming generosity. This is the essential story of the Old Testament; it's a story of a people coming to know and obey a God who chooses them and remains faithful to them even when they are not faithful to him. For they aren't just *any* people, they are *my* people, God says. Through the blood of a covenant and the acceptance of the Law, they bind themselves to God and one another, becoming a people "specially his own" (Dt 26:18).

When God reveals *hesed,* he is not just being nice; he's acting from a commitment that he cannot break. When God shows *hesed,* he isn't just doing random acts of kindness; he is showing love for a people intimately connected to him. In other words, when God acts in this way, he does so, not because of who Israel is, but because of who he is in relation to Israel: faithful and generous. He knows that they are all in this together.

It's with this inherent sense of solidarity that God's forgiveness and patience toward Israel become far more comprehensible. After the Israelites disobeyed God by making a golden calf, God's anger understandably flared up—he had a right to destroy them for so quickly breaking the covenant—but Moses intervened: "Remember your servants Abraham, Isaac, and Israel, and how you swore to them by your own self" (Ex 32:13). Moses does not defend the actions of the people because there is no defense. Rather, he reminds God of who God is. *You are faithful! You made a promise! We are intimately connected to you through this covenant, so in your mercy don't abandon us! Remember the solidarity that we share with one another!* And God relents, time and again, because of his fidelity to them. They are *his* people. His love of what is ultimately tied to himself overrides any sense of needing justice. God and Israel are in this together.

For this reason, God's mercy cannot be a state of passive tolerance—choosing not to punish when it is deserved—but of active intervention. God *does* mercy. When Joseph was in prison, God got involved. When the Israelites were held captive in Egypt, having forgotten the God of their fathers and serving the pharaoh, God sent messengers, performed incredible miracles, and led them to freedom. Over and over again, God is seen feeding the poor, providing strength to armies, nourishing barren lands, and blessing his people with gifts, all leading to the ultimate act of mercy, the Incarnation. In taking on flesh, God so identified with sinners that he allowed himself to be tortured and killed on their behalf, further uniting humanity with himself. Why does God do all of this for a people that is often unfaithful and has no way to pay him back? *Because they are his own. Because they belong to one another with a strong sense of solidarity.* He is faithful to his people and will not let them suffer, even when they deserve it.

This is what Jesus wants from his disciples. He wants people who treat the world the way God treats them—with generosity that overflows even to those who don't deserve it. Followers of Christ do not keep track of the ways they've been hurt by others or ration out their kindness in small doses. There's no need to become judges, deciding what people deserve and when they can have it. Followers of Christ give without counting the cost, sacrifice when there is no apparent benefit for themselves. This kind of mercy is reflected in little acts of kindness, such as letting another driver merge onto the highway; major inconveniences, such as staying late to help a fellow employee finish their work; heroic self-sacrifice, such as giving up on one's own life goals so that another person can flourish; and acts of charity, such as chipping in money so that a friend can make it to a reunion. Jesus tells his disciples that this is how they are to act in the world, generously loving even strangers, even their enemies, even those who betray us and give false witness against us and cause us incredible pain. We are to do this, not because of who they are and what they deserve, but because of who God is and how we are related to him. As beneficiaries of God's manifold grace, we are all in this together as a people who have received what we don't deserve.

When Jesus speaks of the blessedness of those who show mercy, this is what he's talking about. The merciful do not waste their lives holding grudges or losing their tempers over what has been taken from them, but give thanks for the incredible mercy that has already been shown to them. This is not to say that they lack urgency for righteousness or that the work of justice is unimportant—only that they are acutely aware of how desperately the broken need mercy, and that we're committed to one another. Having received God's abundant mercy and so accepted the covenant that binds us together into one human family, how can they not show mercy to other people in need? Blessed are those who treat their neighbor as God has treated them, for they will be shown mercy.

We're in This Together

Growing up, my sisters and I didn't always get along. Normal family struggles. We didn't hate each other and our fights were never particularly feisty, but we did get on each other's nerves, and we did fight. It was not uncommon when we were young for me to make fun of one sister, taunting her when we played sports. She was the far more gifted athlete but couldn't handle a little chatter from her older brother, and so I used that against her. My other sister was equally as vulnerable, only in a physical way. I can hardly think of a time growing up that we played together and she didn't end up injured and crying—something that I always suspected she faked in order to get me in trouble.

There was, of course, that time when we were playing in the snow and I smacked her in the face with a snowball. She was three at the time. I can assure you that her tears were not fake that time.

But before you come rushing to her defense, feeling sorry for her, let me note that this same child was known for *biting* people. Filled with the sort of rage that would scare even an adult three times her size, she learned to deal with her problems by sinking her baby teeth into me and our other sister. Hardly a fitting punishment for hitting your sister in the face with a snowball! As for the sister that I taunted? She was routinely punished for breaking other people's toys. My action figures would have their arms twisted off, my other sister's dolls would be written on, and hers would somehow be left untarnished. Those two were hardly innocent.

Through our teenage years, we had plenty of good moments, but we also had our share of frustrations. I remember how my blood boiled each time one of them told my parents that I had done something wrong, and I suspect that they felt the same when others did it to them. There were moments of passive aggression over who controlled the television, the messiness of our shared bathroom, or whose turn it was to do a particular chore. Publicly we said horrible things to each other in order to get a rise out of the other, and privately we complained to our friends about how terrible our siblings could be. It wasn't all of the time, but there were definitely more than a few instances when we wanted absolutely nothing to do with one another.

But here's the thing: we never gave up on each other. When each of us turned eighteen, no one left the house vowing never to see the others again. Despite our fights, despite our occasional feelings of hatred, we never abandoned each other. Why? Because we're family. Because we're in this together. It may sound cheesy and cliché, but it's the truth. Had the three of us been born into different houses and met at school, there's little chance that we would have liked each other or hung out. What brought us together was not a common view of the world or a similar taste in entertainment. We didn't spend time together because we freely chose one another out of the billions of options for companions around the world. We shared our lives with one another because we were family and had no choice.

That's no insignificant statement: *we've shared our lives together.* Through the years, we've lived in the same places and known the same people; we've vacationed together, watched one another's sports games, and shared countless meals with one another; we were raised by the same parents that we love. Like it or not, we realized that we were in this together, and so we forgave one another—regularly. We overlooked the hurts that were done to us, not because the others deserved our forgiveness or were owed anything in particular, but because that's what you do for your siblings. There is nothing so terrible that any one of us could have done to change the fact that they are my sisters, nothing so unforgivable to dissolve the bond that was given us. While being family doesn't necessarily *require* that people stick together—and many choose not to—for us, it is the fact that we are family that binds us. Solidarity precipitated mercy.

This is not a universal experience. Loyalty to others often has conditions attached. We choose our friends and what we do with our time. If people like us and treat us well, we remain together. If people don't like us and treat us poorly, we move on with our lives. For the most part, there is little culturally binding any of us together, which means there is nothing preventing us from entirely dismissing anyone that doesn't provide us with whatever we're looking for. For people of the world, kindness must be earned.

How different our call is as Christians! Those who know the abundant mercy of God are called to live in solidarity with all of creation, showing mercy even to those who offer us nothing in return. Naturally, this is a task that will require much work.

It begins by remembering that we are ourselves beneficiaries of mercy. I hear people say all the time that life isn't fair, sometimes even that *God* isn't fair. My response is always the same: "You're right! Isn't that wonderful?" Truly, isn't it such great news that God doesn't treat us the way we actually deserve? Can you imagine if we were given God's love only when we earned it? I don't know about you, but my life would be a lot worse off. I've been unfaithful and sinful. Time and again I've turned from God, shaming myself with bad choices. And yet God still loves and cares for me. God still has patience with me and forgives my sins. God still intervenes in my life when I am weak and in need, never forgetting that he is faithful even when I'm not. God is not fair in the slightest. His mercy overflows for his people. As much as we like to think of ourselves as self-made individuals, that we've earned everything we've accomplished through hard work and determination, this is never the case. Not even close. Our very existence is a gift from God and a reminder of his promise to be faithful to us. At the very least, the parable of the unforgiving servant reminds us that the debts owed to us by others pale in comparison to the mercy we've received from God, giving reason for us to show mercy to others.

We must not forget that the promise we've received from God was not made directly with us as individuals, but with God's people as a whole—a reminder of the intimate connection we share with all people. Our very human nature draws us together in community through language and fellowship; we are reared in families and called to societies; the Church is a taste of the kingdom of heaven on earth, a place of mutuality and common worship. Thus, even though each person is afforded individual rights that protect the unique creation that they are, these rights must always be understood as a part of our higher calling to uphold the common good of all. *Who we are individually never supersedes who we are as a united people before our God.*

St. Paul uses various images to highlight this common identity among Christians. Those who partake of the one bread and one body do not remain separate but become what they receive: the Body of Christ. Each has their own function and provides something essential to the body, and none can say that another is of no use. It is why, he writes, "If one part suffers, all the parts suffer with it; if one part is honored, all the parts share its joy" (1 Cor 12:26). Even though it was but one man and one woman who first sinned, all of humanity was cursed, and so even though it was but one man, Jesus Christ, who offered a perfect sacrifice to God, it was all of humanity that was saved. This universal nature we share together in Christ applies to more than just Christians; it applies to Jew and Gentile alike, and even to all of creation. For in Christ "all things were created . . . all things hold together" (Col 1:16–17), and he came to "bring all things into subjection to himself" (Phil 3:21).

What would happen if we truly believed this? How different our world would look if we recognized the common identity we share with all of humanity and chose to live in greater solidarity with our neighbor! What would happen if we treated each other a bit more like family? For truly, that is what we are. Like it or not, we're in this together. All of us. My hope is that, looking to the fidelity our God has to his people, we might begin to care not just about ourselves and our immediate friends, not just about those who like us, not just about how our individual rights have been wronged but also about the life and well-being of our neighbor. How wonderful it would be to show mercy to our neighbor, not because they deserve it or can offer us anything in return, but because we say to ourselves as God does, "Those are my people." The more we can see the common promise that we share with our adversary, the easier it is to show them mercy.

Think about the ways we defend our friends and family members, even when we know that they're wrong. Instead of rushing to judgment, we give them the benefit of the doubt, try to see it from their perspective, empathize with their pain, and may even offer additional chances in forgiveness. We show them a greater sense of tolerance—because they are *our* people. We show them greater forgiveness, letting go of past hurts without retribution. Really, the very thought of causing them pain for past mistakes doesn't even make sense. *That's my sister. That's my friend. I don't want to see her hurt.* Our shared sense of identity mitigates our desire for personal justice because we are intimately aware of the fact that to hurt them is to hurt ourselves. We want not only what's best for me, but what's best for them, for *us*.

The Christian community seeking to live the Beatitudes must always think in terms of *us*. We must do everything we can to expand the sense of solidarity we share with others. As followers of Christ and imitators of God's *hesed*, we are not a people solely focused on the individual feelings of the offended, but a people who understand intimately the interconnectedness of the whole human family. Our justice is thus not interested in retribution—which will bring short-lived satisfaction to some while deepening the pain and division in the community as a whole—it is concerned with reconciliation. We want our whole family to flourish and are willing to do whatever it takes for that to happen.

This is what it means to show mercy. It's not about ignoring justice or allowing ourselves to be treated like doormats; it's about being so permeated by God's fidelity and generosity to humanity that we show the same commitment to others. It's about widening the circle of people we call our own. When we are able to love so inclusively that our generosity knows no bounds, that no one can approach us without receiving our mercy, we are on the way of Beatitude.

Questions for Reflection

1. Who are the people that you would do anything for? How did they come to hold that place in your life? Is there anything that they could do to lose this status with you?

2. Have you ever hurt another person but they immediately forgave you? How did this make you feel to be let off the hook so quickly? Do you forgive others as quickly?

3. Think about all the people you interact with in a day. What do you have in common with them? In what ways are you connected? What can you do to bring a greater bond of unity in the human family?

Practical Acts of Solidarity

*   Make a list of the most diverse people you can from around the world. You do not need to know them personally. For each person, spend some time contemplating how you are already connected to them and what you can do to be in greater solidarity with them.

*   Call someone you haven't talked to in a while. Let them know how important they are to you and ask if there's anything you can do to help them.

*   Do a random chore for someone else. Maybe clean up after them without expecting thanks, or take care of a tedious task they've been assigned. Don't do it because they deserve it or because you want credit for a good deed, but simply because God has already given you more than you deserve.

6. AUTHENTICITY

BLESSED ARE THE PURE OF HEART

Blessed are the pure in heart, for they shall see God.
—Matthew 5:8 (NRSV)

Single-Minded Focus

Before I became a friar, I had the opportunity to work with a Franciscan that I believe is a living saint. At the friars' soup kitchen, he was known by everyone as a simple, caring man who liked to pass out devotional cards with Jesus's name on them and only wore catchy, Christian-themed T-shirts. My favorite was the one that said "Christ the King" in the shape of the Burger King logo. In the many years I've known him, I have never heard him swear or seen him drink and only rarely heard him complain. I don't think it's even possible for him to raise his voice in anger against another. For decades his generosity was so unrelenting and his commitment to the poor so genuine that he developed a serious following among the homeless—not only did they look to him above everyone else when they needed something but many accompanied him all day, helping him with his tasks. Unsurprising to anyone who knows him, I find him to be one of the purest of heart that I have ever met.

In many ways, the polar opposite among the friars is a man currently serving as a pastor of one of our parishes. At least, it would be easy to say so if someone met him only briefly. Not the least bit devotional or sentimental, he is much more likely to be found handing out protest pamphlets at a march for immigration reform or climate change than pious prayer cards. It would not be out of the question for him to be arrested in these situations. He confronts people he disagrees with, challenges authority, angers people with his political homilies, and routinely loses control of his unbridled enthusiasm, inadvertently letting his ideas step on those around him. Oh, and he's been known to drink alcohol from time to time (gasp!). In theory, at least, most people would not immediately think "pure in heart." And yet, he is without a doubt second on my list of the purest of hearts. Let me explain.

The difficulty in understanding this Beatitude, I think, is that the word "purity" has taken on a very particular definition of late, becoming almost exclusively associated with an external sense of moral *cleanliness*. It's about abstinence and self-control, avoiding carnal desires and living without blemish. No sex. No drugs or alcohol. No foul language. Even inappropriate thoughts can lead one astray, and so some treat them as grave sins. It's why churches and schools often bring in professional speakers to talk to students about chastity; theology-of-the-body study groups meet to learn more about the theological purpose of sexuality; in the confessional, the most common sin I hear is that of "impure thoughts and actions," a euphemism for the inappropriate use of one's body. Coming-of-age rituals are often fused with purity pledges and pledges against alcohol; even the use of chapel veils and scapulars—practices that are becoming very popular in parts of the Church—is an effort by some members of the faithful to become more *pure*.

In itself, there's nothing wrong with any of this. It is a wholly good desire to want to abstain from promiscuity and live a moral life. Jesus forgives the woman caught in adultery but tells her to sin no more. He repeatedly affirms the importance of the Ten Commandments in his teachings. St. Paul speaks frequently about the dangers of the flesh and the allurements of the world, encouraging those who cannot remain chaste to marry lest they fall into grave sin. He warns the Corinthians that damnation befalls the impure: "Do not be deceived; neither fornicators nor idolaters nor adulterers nor boy prostitutes nor sodomites nor thieves nor the greedy nor drunkards nor slanderers nor robbers will inherit the kingdom of God" (1 Cor 6:9–10). To remain morally pure—that is, free of contact with unclean actions and people—seems paramount.

And yet, Jesus is routinely found associating with the "unclean." At a dinner with Simon, he allows the sinful woman to bathe his feet in tears even while the Pharisee judges him. He eats with tax collectors and prostitutes, relating with them on a familial level. He does not heal the blind and the lepers from afar; he touches them—in one instance, using his own spit mixed with mud. He does not condemn the woman at the well, even though she is shunned by her village; instead, he offers her the chance to be a prophet for the Gospel. Mary Magdalene, who was once possessed by seven demons, becomes the first to believe in the Resurrection and announces it to the other disciples. And after all of this, when his disciples fail to keep the tradition of the elders, ritually washing before meals, Jesus does not correct them. In fact, he corrects those who criticize him.

In trying to grasp what Jesus means by pure of heart, this might be the most telling evidence of all. Notice how he interacts with the Pharisees. In the whole of the ancient world, the

Pharisees best exemplified ritualistic moral purity—an intent focus on cleanliness and adherence to external law—and yet they were the ones most harshly criticized by Jesus. The fact that they fasted regularly, gave alms in large measure, and prayed throughout the day does not impress Jesus one bit. They turned from all impurities that would exclude them from Temple worship, strictly observing the washings and sacrifices necessary to remedy any mistakes, and yet he condemns them. Their vigor for purity, believe it or not, disgusts Jesus.

The reason for this, we well know, is that they are hypocritical. They profess one thing with their lips and another with their hearts. They perform acts to be seen and heard, to bring acclaim among their peers, without much care for their relationship with God and neighbor. Like actors in a play, they know all of the lines and are always in the right place, but their lives are nothing more than show. Their hearts are divided, mixed between competing desires, focused on more than just God. In other words, their hearts are *impure*.

Too often, the problem with our understanding of purity— and why the second friar I mentioned would not register as pure of heart for most—is that we treat it as synonymous with cleanliness when Jesus actually intends it as "undivided." While he is certainly intent on his followers observing the commandments and living moral lives, the lack of external blemishes is not the mark of a true disciple: a focused, devoted heart is. The one with a pure heart is one whose intentions match their actions, who present themselves exactly as they are. As the old saying goes, "What you see is what you get." There's no guile, no ulterior motives, no clandestine hobbies or double life. At the center of who they are is a desire to please God and serve their neighbor, as well as an undeniable confidence in who they are and what they are to do. This is what makes someone a blessed disciple and what makes the Pharisees so repugnant.

This perspective on purity is evident in the way the Sermon on the Mount progresses in the verses that follow the Beatitudes. As soon as Jesus finishes listing the eight conditions of blessedness, he exhorts his followers to go beyond the external law and to reform their inner motivations. It is not enough merely to avoid acts of murder, adultery, false witness, and retaliation—external acts of the law—one must go deeper, removing the anger, lust, deceit, and hatred inside oneself that lead to impure actions. The same is true even of naturally good actions. It is not enough merely to give alms, pray, and fast—external acts of the law—it matters *how* and *why* one performs these acts. In another sermon toward the end of the gospel, Jesus teaches that "it is not what enters one's mouth that defiles that person; but what comes out of the mouth is what defiles one. . . . For from the heart come evil thoughts, murder, adultery, unchastity, theft, false witness, blasphemy" (Mt 15:11, 19). The intention of the heart defines a person's standing with God.

This is what makes the two friars I wrote about at the beginning of this chapter pure of heart. One has devoted his life to direct service of the poor while the other is committed to bringing about societal change, but both have a singular dedication to the kingdom of heaven. It's all they care about. It's all they *live* for. While neither is without blemish or personal idiosyncrasies, and while their passion has stepped on more than a few toes, I'm not sure there's a person in the world who could question their intentions. Never in my life have I met two people less driven by their egos. Truly, they live without guile. It is about the mission of Christ. Period. If that means admitting a mistake, they do it. If it means letting someone else take the lead, they do it. If it means collaborating with their enemies and welcoming new people into the fold, they do it. All while smiling and laughing through the day.

And that's the fruit of it. That's the incredible witness to this Beatitude they share. Given the frustrating work that these men do, it would be completely understandable if they lost their temper from time to time. No one would fault them for periods of low enthusiasm and lack of hope. How can you serve the chronically poor for decades, dedicate your life to enacting change in something so discouraging as the American political system, and not grow a bit depressed? But they rarely show it. In the years that I've known them, I have seen them each genuinely angry only once. Even when discussing terrible tragedies of human suffering or sharing about true enemies to the Gospel, they do not lose their composure, lash out, crumble, or become cynical. All I ever see is the patient joy of men who see God in all that they do.

For me, it's the reason that some people see miracles and others don't. Those who do not have faith, or whose faith is split between two worlds, will always come up with reasons to doubt what they see. *It could have been a coincidence. I was mistaken. That's not God, it's just my mind playing tricks on me.* Those who are torn between many allegiances will find themselves weighed down with doubt, crushed by cynicism, or left debilitated by a bevy of choices. Not so for the pure of heart. In their heart of hearts they know that God is real, that the created order is good, that God actually mediates his presence through the physical world, and that everything has the capacity for redemption. When goodness presents itself, how can they *not* see God? When they encounter challenging people or situations, how can they *not* hold on to hope? Because of their purity of heart, they can see God in everything they do.

And there it is. When Jesus speaks of the blessedness of the pure in heart, this is what he's talking about. They will see God because it is the natural conclusion of living with a single-minded focus—if serving God in one's neighbor is the only desire of one's heart, then God in one's neighbor is all they'll see. Really, how could they see anything *but* God? When one is dedicated wholly and completely to the mission of Christ, there is no temptation for personal gain, no wounded ego to be healed, no insecure doubts to attend to. The pure of heart live without ulterior motives or wayward desires. Blessed are those who desire nothing but the kingdom, for they shall see God.

The Only Opinion That Matters

Walk through the checkout lane at any grocery store or gas station and you'll find countless magazines touting celebrity gossip, fashion trends, glamorous lifestyles, and beauty tips. The covers always display beautiful people—through the magic of photo editing literally flawless in appearance—subtly (or sometimes not so subtly) setting a standard for how the rest of us should look. And it works. Despite recent efforts to expose the artificial nature of these images and demand more natural representations of the human body, these images have a strong hold on many people. Studies have shown that a significant number of women, and a growing number of men, have problems with body image and self-esteem. They believe they should look like the images on magazine covers and work to conform to that unrealistic standard. They buy expensive beauty products, go on extreme diets, and some subject themselves to cosmetic surgeries to drastically alter their appearance. Why? Because they want to be accepted by the world.

I have been fortunate not to have struggled much with issues of body image or self-esteem like so many others. My intent is not to trivialize the issue, but to get to the heart of what causes people so much pain. For many, it's not about beauty in itself, something that could be dismissed as superficial, but about the worth of one's identity. Really, it doesn't matter if we're talking about outward appearance, job performance, personal wealth, shoe size, or the number of letters in one's last name—the feeling of not being accepted by another because of a personal trait is painful. No one wants to be excluded or rejected in any situation, and so the pressure to conform to the standards of the world weighs upon us, even if we're not fully conscious of it.

As someone who spends a significant amount of time consuming content on social media, I experience this pressure every day. Like the glamour magazines, social media presents me with a constant barrage of images—in this case, of what a priest or Christian is supposed to be like, how I am to act, what I'm supposed to be thinking. As odd as it may sound, there are definitely "celebrities" and "models" in the religious world that set a standard, implicitly pressuring others to conform. The goal may be different—holiness and devotion rather than outward beauty and fashion—but I would argue that the same pressure exists: wanting to be accepted by others, we evaluate our lives against theirs and work to emulate them. We focus less on who we are and more on those we think we want to become.

As a content *creator*, I feel this pressure actively. Unlike magazines that present information in one direction only, social media is interactive. When I post content, people *respond*. Statistics. Likes. Comments. Reposts. Reviews. Almost instantly, my work and life are evaluated by the world. Sometimes a video will be immensely popular, racking up hundreds of thousands of views and innumerable comments to the tune of, "You're so great! You really helped me with this!" At other times, my inbox is flooded with derogatory attacks on my character while my content is spread by those who wish only to make fun of me. Nearly every day, I hear a cacophony of voices telling me who I am and what I'm worth.

When I'm at my best, grounded in what matters, none of this means much. I evangelize and catechize online because that's what I'm called to do. I believe in the content, work hard on what I want to say, and stand by it, regardless of how it is accepted. The work of the Gospel is its own reward.

Unfortunately, I'm not always at my best. Like everyone, there is a part of me that does care what others think of me and that desires to be liked by the world, and sometimes this value rises to the top. When this happens, the voices are hard to ignore. Positive comments offer validation and leave me thinking that I'm doing great work. Negative attacks either harden my attitude against the world or downright demoralize me, leaving me to believe that my work is useless. Statistics become paramount, tricking me into thinking that the number of views is directly related to the quality of the content. This in turn leads to the dangerous temptation of conforming the content to the result, creating what will produce the most views and avoiding what won't be popular. Why? Because the desire to be accepted by the world sometimes overrides my desire to be faithful to the Gospel. When this happens—when my identity becomes confused and my heart becomes mixed with multiple intentions—everything falls apart.

The problem with serving two masters is that we can never give either one our entire heart. As Jesus says, you will either "hate one and love the other, or be devoted to one and despise the other" (Mt 6:24). As much as the world likes to tell us that we can have it all, it's simply not true. Attention given to the values of the world is attention not given to God. When we live with one foot in the Church and another trying to serve the world, when our hearts are mixed or confused rather than purely focused on God, the division within us prevents us from fully living the Gospel.

I see this periodically in the ways that church people judge the work of the Gospel by the standards of earthly success. When we evaluate the life of a parish, it's all about Mass attendance and collection numbers. In a more general sense, it's about doing and accomplishing. How many programs do we have, and how many people walk through the doors each day? There's nothing wrong with tracking these numbers as a by-product of our work—one would hope that the work of the Gospel also produces the earthly success of numbers and financial stability. The problem is that we often confuse the by-product with the goal, serving the master of earthly success rather than the master of the Gospel. When this happens, our preaching reflects a tension between the desire to say what is true and the desire to say what is popular; our activities calendar reflects a tension between what will develop lifelong disciples and what is fun; our social outreach reflects a tension between the demands of the Gospel and the fear of upsetting donors. At work are two identities in conflict and two masters we seek to please. We may choose God much of the time, even *most* of the time, but as long as our hearts are mixed with a desire for earthly success, there will always be something holding us back from true service to the Gospel.

The same can be said of those religious who get caught up seeking the acclaim of the secular world. For whatever reason, they feel validated when a celebrity takes up Christianity or includes faith in an interview. Finding the favor of *The New York Times* matters to them, and being criticized by its opinion section is an indictment of our faith. I'm always amazed how giddy some get when an atheist or secular humanist publicly agrees, even mildly, with a stance of the Church; they are praised and invited to speak on behalf of the Church's position, as if being an outsider makes one's stance more compelling to the world. Again, in itself, none of this is a bad thing. Jesus told his disciples to evangelize the whole world, and so it should bring us great joy when the secular world comes to accept what we believe. But it can't be our utmost goal. The acclaim of outsiders is the by-product of a holy life, not the goal. To flip these around would be to replace our master with another, conflicting our mission. For if acclaim is what we desire, we will be tempted to oversimplify our beliefs to be a bit more generic and thus relatable; to overlook some crucial doctrines to be more inclusive and worldly; to go along with trends and fads to appear more relevant; or even to act as the world does so that the world will praise us. We may choose God much of the time, even *most* of the time, but as long as our hearts are mixed with a desire for secular acclaim, there will always be something holding us back from true service to the Gospel.

If we look at the history of Christianity, it is difficult to ignore the way that our desire for power has undermined the mission of Christ. From the time of Constantine to the present world of politics, there have been Christians torn between the desire to live in humble service to the Gospel and the desire to spread the reach of the Church through political or social power. While few today would suggest returning to a time when the Church coerced its enemies through actual violence, many still seem to believe that wielding political, social, or economic power is essential to the kingdom of heaven. "Think about all we could do if we got a Christian elected president! Think about the effect we could have if we had more money!" And so begins our service to yet another master, a desire that divides our hearts. At times the desires may appear to overlap—we are using our power *for* God, right?—but it is the case with all power that one has to fight to obtain it and fight to keep it, leaving us in more than a few questionable positions.

Even more than that, one has to question if the idea of a powerful Christian isn't self-contradictory, undermining the very witness of Christ. If our intention to do something *for* God ends up compromising our place *in* God, have we not confused our values? I say it once more, we may choose God much of the time, even *most* of the time, but as long as our hearts are mixed with a desire for power, there will always be something holding us back from true service to the Gospel.

If we want to continue as disciples of Christ, we must purify our hearts. We must purge from them any false identities or disparate desires that divide us and leave us unsure of what we are to do. There is only one God, one mission of Christ that deserves our utmost attention, and this must be what defines us above all else.

If we don't know how to get there, I recommend imitating one of the purest hearts who ever lived, St. Francis of Assisi. In his work called *Admonitions*, proverb-like bits of advice for the brothers struggling to live the Gospel, he wrote one of my favorite lines in all of Christianity: "What a man is in the sight of God, so much he is, and no more." Is there anything more grounding and reassuring than this? What St. Francis reminded his brothers of, and what we need to remind the world of, is that no one's opinion of us matters one bit next to the opinion of God. The world will try to tell us who we are. Magazines will try to tell us what is beautiful. Random accounts on social media will try to define our worth. Everyone we meet for the rest of our lives—from our family members to our worst enemies—will have an opinion of us and our path in life, pulling us in every direction. But at the end of the day, all that matters is who we are in the sight of God. All that matters is who God created us and loves us to be.

This is what it means to be pure in heart. It's not about abstinence or being in control, hiding from what is unclean or being prudish. It's about knowing who we are and where we're going. It's about living with firm conviction for the mission of Christ because we know there is nothing that we could ever want more. When we are able to live with such singular focus on Christ that nothing could ever tempt us to stray from it, we are on the way of Beatitude.

Questions for Reflection

1. Do you live with single-minded focus, or are you scattered with many goals? What causes you to lose focus? What helps you get back on track?

2. Whose opinion of you matters? Even if God's is the most important or defining one, chances are you are affected by what others say of you. What do they say, and how do you respond?

3. Who are you in the sight of God? You were created different from anyone else that has ever lived, destined for a unique purpose. How do you think God sees you, and how does this compare to how you see yourself?

Practical Acts of Authenticity

- Make a mission statement for yourself. Define who you are, what you stand for, and what vocation you have in building up the kingdom of heaven. In everything you do, ask yourself, *Does this fit with my mission statement?* and then respond accordingly.

- When someone shares their opinion of you, good or bad, take it to prayer. Ask God if this voice is worth listening to. Be completely honest with yourself, accepting compliments or criticisms when valid.

- When you go to the Sacrament of Reconciliation, be sure to think of the many ways you bring life into the world as well as the areas where you have fallen. Too often we focus exclusively on our sins, potentially leading us to think that this is all we are.

7. LIBERATION

BLESSED ARE THE PEACEMAKERS

Blessed are the peacemakers, for they will be called children of God.

—Matthew 5:9

If You Want Peace, Work for Justice

Of the many stories told of St. Francis, few have captured the imagination of his devotees quite like the tale of the Wolf of Gubbio. According to the legend, a wolf began terrorizing the inhabitants of a small Italian city, first attacking their livestock, then the people themselves. The wolf was so fierce that no attempt to kill it was ever successful, and the people lived in such fear that they never left the city walls. Francis decided to do something about it. Against the warnings of the terrified towns-people, he made the Sign of the Cross and left the city walls in search of the wolf. Eventually, the two met in what should have been a bloody showdown—the wolf charged at Francis with mouth open, ready to attack as it normally did—but no blood was shed. Francis made the Sign of the Cross again and shouted at the wolf, commanding that, in the name of Christ, it was to harm the city no more. He admonished the wolf for its sins, clearly stating the ways that it had acted against God and neighbor. And just like that, the wolf fell docile! It was an extraordinary sight that left his companions speechless.

But Francis was not done yet. Recognizing that the wolf was hungry, and that this dire state had contributed to its sinful behavior, Francis promised to bring peace to the wolf as well. If it agreed not to attack the townspeople or steal their livestock, Francis would guarantee that the wolf was never chased or attacked again, and that food would be provided to it each day. Bowing its head and offering its paw, the wolf agreed, and from that point on, the wolf and townspeople lived in peace. It became such a welcome visitor to the city that, upon its death a few years later, the people greatly mourned the loss of the wolf.

It's no wonder this story has survived for centuries. I've heard it told in a variety of ways and have seen it performed by schoolchildren. For many, it is St. Francis at his absolute best. The story, of course, is the work of hagiography, folklore told of a saint to promote faith and devotion; few would seriously claim that such an anthropomorphic wolf really existed or that Francis literally facilitated peace between a city and a wolf. But that doesn't mean the story isn't true. The reason it lives on so many centuries later is that it depicts Francis as he fundamentally was: a peacemaker. However fantastic it may appear, the story of the Wolf of Gubbio provides an authentically Franciscan approach to the world and a number of insights for disciples striving to live the Beatitudes.

We begin with the simple fact that Francis got involved at all. How easy it would have been for him to remain within the city walls. Chances are, he could have fled the city fast enough to evade the wolf, forgetting the city's problem as he continued on with his life. It would have provided him much greater inner peace to avoid the stress of confrontation and danger of violence. But Francis didn't choose this option. He couldn't stand idly by while people lived in fear and injustice reigned. The human family was tearing apart, and so he set aside his desire for tranquility, took up the risk of experiencing violence, and worked for reconciliation. He decided to *make* peace.

This is the approach to peace of which Jesus speaks in the seventh Beatitude. Notice that he does not say that those who live *in* peace are blessed. It's not about being a *lover* of peace. Avoiding violence and living without conflict certainly provide an enjoyable existence, but this behavior in itself hardly seems in line with the counterintuitive nature of the rest of the Beatitudes. Rather, Jesus's focus is, once again, not on the state of one's life but on the motivation that defines one's life. It's not about receiving or enjoying peace, it's about going out of one's way—even giving up safety and comfort—in order to *make* peace.

In our world today, we might look to the issue of combatting racism for an example of this distinction. In the work of racial equality, many are "nonracist"—those who hold no discernible prejudice against others based on race and view racial discrimination as a blight on the human family. On the whole, they're concerned for people of other races and wish that everyone could live in peace. But it remains just a wish. Their approach to racism is that of passivity; they are disgusted enough by the status quo to be morally against it but not enough to really get involved. They want peace but are not willing to work for it. In other words, they're not a part of the problem, but they're also not part of the solution. To be a peace*maker*, we must shift our focus to being "antiracists"—people who are against racism to the point that they are willing to make sacrifices to bring an end to it. It's about getting involved, about actively taking risks and changing one's life. For those who desire to make peace above all, these sacrifices are worth it. As Jesus taught and Francis displayed, the blessed disciples do not passively hope for peace, they make it happen.

Of course, this is never something that any of us does on our own. The true bringer of peace knows that nothing is possible without the work of the Prince of Peace, Jesus. When Francis set off on his mission, what did he do? He made the Sign of the Cross. When he approached the wolf, what did he do? He made the Sign of the Cross. This act is not to be confused with magical or superstitious gestures, as if the symbol in itself has power to control others. Rather, what it shows is that everything Francis did was grounded in faith. He knew that if reconciliation was to come from his work, it wasn't because of his efforts alone. Jesus was at work in him.

Sadly, this is something that humanity forgets from time to time. I think of the disciples' inability to cast the demon out of the boy. After Jesus steps in and does it for them, he reveals where they went wrong: "This kind can only come out through prayer" (Mk 9:29). The disciples were attempting to take on the devil and save a boy's life, yet they didn't consider it important enough to pray first! How absolutely illogical, and yet how often I do the same in my own life. Skilled in many ways, I can easily forget where those skills came from and why I was given them. At times, I find myself slipping into a self-reliant attitude of "I can do this on my own." I never go as far as to say that I'm better without God, but really, what's the difference between that and trying to accomplish important tasks without prayer? Francis knew that this wasn't possible, and so should we.

It was from this place of absolute grounding in God that Francis was able to do what might seem impossible: he confronted a ravaging wolf and spoke truth to power. Francis didn't hesitate, and the story gives no indication that he feared for his own life. Clearly and emphatically, he listed the sins of the wolf and commanded that it change. He stood up to the evil within the wolf and denounced it directly. The truth mattered more than his own life; justice for the people determined his actions. It wouldn't have mattered if it had been a wolf, a king, his brother, or the devil himself, Francis could not have remained silent when peace was at stake. The makers of peace do not tolerate injustice—they confront it.

For many, this example of peacemaking might seem a bit unsettling and difficult to reconcile with our otherwise gentle image of the animal-loving saint. A confrontational, critical attitude appears entirely antithetical to the work of peace. And yet, that is precisely how Jesus acts on numerous occasions with the Pharisees, clearly naming their sins; it's how he treats the money changers in the Temple when he flips their tables; in his discourse immediately following the Sermon on the Mount, he tells the disciples, "Do not think that I have come to bring peace upon the earth. I have come to bring not peace but the sword" (Mt 10:34). Hardly images of a nice, gentle person. Then again, one has to wonder why we would expect this from Jesus in the first place.

When Jesus speaks of peace, he is not talking about manners or niceties, working to keep everyone comfortable in the way things are. Instead, he speaks of the ancient Hebrew *shalom*, a call to avoid violence, yes, but more importantly, a call to uphold the goodness of the whole person and to promote everything that contributes to a good life. It's about truth. It's about justice. When someone fundamentally challenges the truth of the Gospel or undermines the justice of society, it benefits no one to be "nice," to allow them to continue to harm others and themselves. It may appear divisive, but correcting someone in grave error—freeing them from the peril that they inflict upon the world and their own souls—is one of the most charitable, peaceful things one can do.

I think of the many ways the Church has been perceived as a threat in recent decades because of its work for economic justice. In our care for the poor and oppressed, we have consistently demanded a living wage for workers, supported laborers in their right to unionize, and even allowed strikes as a means of last resort. Popes have repeatedly insisted for two centuries that the universal destination of goods is an imperative greater than one's right to private property, and that the rich have a moral obligation to distribute their wealth for the good of all. In doing so, some have criticized us for instigating conflicts and stirring up trouble. Some think that we advocate stealing what is rightfully theirs. But what can we say? When someone's wealth comes as a result of abusing the poor and neglecting the demands of justice, it does not rightfully belong to them, and allowing them to continue uncorrected hurts everyone. Truly, it is their injustice that is divisive, not our admonishment. Silence in this situation may be "nice," but it brings no lasting peace for anyone.

For what does the prophet Isaiah say? "The work of justice will be peace; the effect of justice, calm and security forever" (Is 32:17). Put another way, St. Paul VI famously proclaimed, "If you want peace, work for justice." Acts of physical violence don't come out of nowhere. They're the result of a people enduring countless acts of moral violence before finally deciding they've had enough. For many, violence is an act of last resort, an explosion of desperation from a people who have no recourse to proper protections. In the struggles of the world, it is often the poor or marginalized who draw first blood, engaging in riots and destructive acts of violence, but can we really say that these are unprovoked? Were they not attacked first? The seeds of their violence were planted by the innumerable acts of injustice they had to endure at the hands of others. To look only at violence without considering what caused it will always fail to bring true peace. Like Jesus and St. Francis, we must stand up to evildoers, clearly name their sins, and demand justice.

That is, if we demand justice *for all*. We might be unsettled by the directness of Francis's words, but at no point did he show hate toward the wolf. He made no attempt to conquer or humiliate it. In what can only be described as quintessential St. Francis, he recognized the wolf as a brother, bruised and broken, in need of justice as were the townspeople. He saw that the wolf acted violently, not because it was evil in itself, but because it was hungry. And so, recognizing a desperate need in one of God's creatures, he brokered a deal: feed the wolf and peace will be felt by all. In the end, what brought about peace for the people wasn't a larger weapon or severe punishment; it was genuine care for the enemy.

What is so often overlooked in our quest for justice is the fact that those who commit injustice, like the wolf, may be doing so because they are trapped in sin themselves. While it is true that we are all capable of evil and some do truly horrible things, I simply cannot believe that anyone chooses evil as an end in itself. They choose evil, not because it brings them happiness or fulfillment, but because they have a distorted sense of the good. They cannot see the fullness of good, the effects of their actions, or the futility of their choices. They seek what they believe will bring them happiness or comfort in the moment, but it only temporarily alleviates their hunger. It's possible that people attack because they seek safety and are afraid of being attacked themselves. Maybe they perpetuate a system of injustice because that's the only world that they can fathom and there's no way for them to get out. This is not to let people off the hook for their evil deeds or to suggest that good intentions make up for hurting others. Rather, it is a reminder that people are more complicated than a mere good/evil dichotomy. Even evildoers might be victims in need of help. To treat them like they treat others seems right and just at first, but it saves no one. It continues the cycle of violence and makes us just like them. The only way out, for both the evildoer and victim, is love.

When Jesus speaks of the blessedness of peacemakers, this is what he means: they don't just avoid violence, they commit their lives to freeing those trapped by it. They see evil, and instead of trying to destroy their enemy, as their enemy has tried to do to them, they love. Desiring peace and justice for all of God's creatures, not just themselves, they risk their own comfort, ground themselves in prayer, and speak truth to power, all the while caring for evildoers as they would their friends. Blessed are those who liberate their enemies, for they will be children of God.

Hate Doesn't Evangelize

The world is not left wanting for revenge movies. Every year, Hollywood churns out a new version of the same story. It might be a woman shot and left for dead at her own wedding (*Kill Bill*), a former assassin whose car is stolen and dog killed (*John Wick*), or a Roman general who survives a coup attempt (*Gladiator*), but the end result is always the same: a wronged, highly dangerous person returns from obscurity to gain retribution for what was done to them. They suffered injustice, and someone must pay!

Generally speaking, these movies are successful at the box office. Not only do they provide the audience with two hours of whirlwind action and entertainment, there's just something about them, I have to admit, that is satisfying to the viewer. Justice is served. The bad people are punished and the wronged are vindicated. In a world where evil so often seems to triumph and evildoers get away with causing harm in the lives of the innocent, movies like these offer a fantasy escape, a taste of a world in which the difference between the good guys and bad guys is clear-cut, and the road to justice is simple: annihilate your enemies.

But what sort of justice are we really talking about here? Skip the first act of any of these movies and what do you see? A hate-filled rampage involving the humiliation or death of countless people. Even in movies where the one seeking revenge doesn't use violence—as in, say, a high-school movie about getting back at the bully or a heist movie trying to bankrupt a billionaire—the main desire of the protagonist is not to make their own life any better; it's to make another's life worse. They seek to harm. If we forget that they were hurt first and overlook the fact that they have a charming personality on camera—in other words, if we look at their actions and motivations in themselves—what we see is repugnant. Murder. Abuse. Destruction. Humiliation. Regardless of what was done to them first, it is difficult to see how a desire to cause this sort of pain in the human family could ever come close to true justice.

Unfortunately, I see this sort of attitude on display regularly in our Church and world. It may not involve guns or swords, but it's the same hatred that fuels our movie protagonists, the same desire to separate and destroy. Snide remarks fly through social media. Passive aggression pervades family life. Political adversaries escalate attack ads against one another. Back and forth we go. From a place of hurt, we can feel justified in acting nastily. Judgment. Insults. Accusations. Condemnations. In my frequent interactions with people online, I have seen and received it all from self-proclaimed faithful Christians. Even among the followers of Jesus, there are plenty who live with an "us and them" attitude, dividing the human family between friend and enemy.

The sad irony of acts like these is that many people honestly believe that they are doing nothing more than what Francis did with the wolf: instructing the ignorant and admonishing the sinner. And maybe that is the case for some; there is plenty of error on social media, and someone needs to bring truth to light. In my experience, though, there are far more wolves than Francises, people looking to destroy rather than reconcile. This is a problem.

When hatred is what motivates us, it can be all too easy to convince ourselves that we are on a holy mission, that we are the good guys taking on the bad guys, just like in the movies. We are so sure of this fact and so desperate to achieve our mission that we begin to make compromises, justifying our nasty behavior as necessary for the greater good. It's righteous anger, we say. Evil has no rights, we tell ourselves, and so evildoers deserve what they get. Our harsh behavior gives us a rush of energy, a sense of power, a momentary feeling of satisfaction in having humiliated our enemy, owning them in a big way.

But then what? After the dust settles, can we declare victory? Hardly. What we find in nearly every one of these cases is that our enemies still remain, likely more emboldened in their hatred for us than they were before. Worse than that, our hatred and rage will eventually have an effect on us. The more time we spend compromising our values to conquer our perceived enemies, the more likely it is that we'll become the very thing we claim to stand against: people of darkness. As in the revenge movies, our actions may have started as righteous anger and seemed along the way to be justified, but at some point we'll realize that we've simply spent our time judging, condemning, dividing, and causing harm, all in the name of Jesus Christ, who stands against it all. In our pursuit to destroy evil, we become evil ourselves; in our desire to promote Christian values, we cease to follow Christ.

For Christians, the ends never justify the means. Never. It doesn't matter if we're going up against a wolf, a politician, a family member, or the devil himself, when we approach our enemy in an attempt to destroy them, when we are motivated by hate, when we allow ourselves to become so enflamed by an issue that we're willing to ignore the commands of Christ to love our neighbor and not to judge, we will *always* lose. Why? Because we will have ceased to be that which we proclaim: a people of peace.

As much as some try, you can't evangelize with hate. You can't profess to believe in a God of humility, peace, and love while exhibiting none of those characteristics yourself. Some will say that "truth is truth," that it doesn't matter how we say something about Christ, but I don't agree. Just as it's illogical to profess love without truth—a stance that would amount to nothing more than sentimentality—so, too, is it illogical for a Christian to profess truth without love. For a Christian, what is the truth that we profess *but* the love of Christ? The work of evangelization cannot be true if it lacks love. Remember what St. Paul writes in his first letter to the Corinthians: "If I speak in human and angelic tongues. . . if I have the gift of prophecy and comprehend all mysteries and all knowledge; if I have faith so as to move mountains. . . if I give away everything I own, and if I hand my body over so that I may boast but do not have love, I gain nothing" (1 Cor 13:1–3). It doesn't matter how perfectly we teach the doctrines of the Church, recount the miracles of Jesus, or apply the dictates of canon law. If we do so with hate in our hearts in order to destroy our enemy, we undermine everything that is truthful about what we say.

The only thing that evangelizes is love. The only thing that will ever change someone's mind, cause them to turn from their evil ways, accept Jesus into their lives, and become a peacemaker themselves is love. If we want to make peace in our world, we must put down our weapons and take up the Cross. How do we do this? By following St. Francis's example with the wolf.

It begins with a genuine desire to get involved. We have to *want* to make peace. Just as Francis had the opportunity to hide behind the walls or flee the city, we can choose to not care. And we do, all of the time. In the past few years, I have been dumbfounded by the number of Christians who have told me that they have no interest in loving their enemy. Just like that. They've watched what *those* people have done in politics, what *that* segment of the Church is advocating for, and they want nothing to do with it. What they live with is not the fiery hate of condemnation, but the stone-cold hate of dismissal. They care so little about a person that they can't even be bothered to try. Regrettably, I know that I have taken this approach even with some of the men I've lived with as a friar. Deeming them to be lazy, inconsiderate, hypocritical, or downright mean, I have at times chosen to give up caring. Why should I continue to try to make peace with them when they treat me like this? Why make any effort to love them when they provide absolutely nothing to the community? It's an understandable approach for the world. It's nowhere close to acceptable as the attitude of those of us called by baptism to be peacemakers.

Sometimes, it may seem impossible to care for someone who causes us so much harm. If this is the case, we must rely on Francis's second step: turning to prayer. It might sound obvious, but I'm always struck by how little people pray for their enemies. They will come to Confession sharing the hate they feel at the horrible things people have done to them and I always ask, "Have you prayed for this person?" More times than not, you would think I had just personally attacked them and sided with their enemy. The thought of praying for our enemies rarely crosses our minds. When we think of prayer, we think about blessings for the ones we love, almost as if prayer is a reward for the good people. This is not what we want for our enemies! We want them to suffer! But who needs prayers more than those trapped in sin? Surely, even on our worst days, we do not wish sin on our enemies. We want them to convert their hearts. But believing that we can change the heart of an unrepentant sinner is as crazy as thinking we can tame a ravenous wolf! We know that we can't do it on our own, and so we must go to the one who can: Jesus.

But we don't just go to Jesus in the hope that the sinner will change. One of the recommendations I often give in the confessional is that the penitent pray for their enemies, not so much that their enemy will conform to our perfect notion of sainthood, but so that *we* can change in the way that we see them. Our faith tells us that each and every creature bears the mark of God; we know that every human, no matter how tarnished with sin, is created in the image and likeness of God. There is nothing we could ever do to lose the love of Christ because Christ can see who we are beneath our brokenness. What if we could look at our enemies this way? Without condoning their sins or diminishing the need for justice, what if we could look at our enemies and see the goodness within them that Jesus loves? Given the resentment we bear toward those who have hurt us, it may seem like an impossible task, but it's one that a peacemaker willingly takes on.

And it's imperative that we do. As we approach step three—striking up the courage to confront our enemies and admonish them for their sins—it's easy to see how this can go terribly wrong without a Christlike disposition. As we've seen, people admonish one another all of the time from a disposition of hate, seeking to destroy their enemy, and it often results in disaster. Without a desire to make peace, without Christ guiding the way, no correction will make a difference, no matter how true it is.

But imagine if we approached our enemy having seen them as Christ does. Imagine if, like Francis, we saw them as our brother or sister in Christ, someone we actually cared about.

Imagine if, anticipating step four, we recognized that our enemy is just as much a victim as an evildoer, trapped in their sin with no way out. Imagine if, remembering our own sinfulness, we realized that we are just as much in need of saving as the person before us, that our own faults sometimes get in the way of learning from the truth and goodness already present in them. Our approach to our enemies might be a little different. Rather than trying to destroy them, giving them what we think they deserve, we might look with compassion upon them, ashamed of ourselves that we ever considered hurting someone in such a hopeless position, and instead set as our utmost goal the need to walk together as one people. How we would resemble children of God when that happens!

This is what it means to be a peacemaker. It's not just about avoiding violence and keeping our inner calm; it's about being so absolutely committed to the justice of the kingdom that we can't bear to see even our enemies suffer. Having felt the hopelessness of sin and having been stuck in the cycle of violence ourselves, we no longer seek revenge on our enemies because we know what pain they feel. All we can feel is pity, resolving ourselves to set them free. When we can approach those who harm us with compassion, risking our own life and comfort for the justice of all, we are on the way of Beatitude.

Questions for Reflection

1. Think about the people you struggle to get along with. Do you even want to get along with them? If not, what is preventing you from wanting to reconcile with your brother or sister?

2. Who in your life needs someone to stand up to them and set them free from their bad behavior? How might you

approach them lovingly? What will make them receptive to hearing what you have to say?

3. Have you ever sought revenge for wrongs done to you? Did it bring satisfaction or make the situation worse? How might you have been able to break the cycle of violence and bring liberation to everyone involved?

Practical Acts of Liberation

- The next time you get in a fight with someone, try to get beneath the anger. Imagine what it's like to be them. Are they dealing with pain or trauma that you might be able to alleviate?

- Pray for someone who causes you great distress. Ask God to give you the ability to see what God loves so much about them.

- Show someone you think of as an enemy a random act of kindness. The relationship may not be reconciled in a day, but a little patience and mercy can be the sort of olive branch that entirely shifts the dynamic.

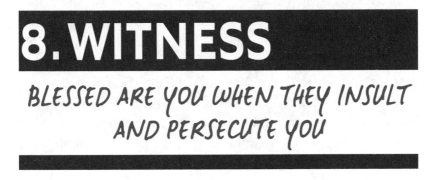

8. WITNESS

BLESSED ARE YOU WHEN THEY INSULT AND PERSECUTE YOU

> Blessed are you when they insult you and persecute you
> and utter every kind of evil against you because of me.
> Rejoice and be glad, for your reward will be great in heaven.
> —Matthew 5:11–12

The Sting of Rejection

I heard my name called over the airport loudspeaker just as I was arriving at my gate. I hurried to speak to the woman at the desk. *Is there an issue? Am I getting bumped?* It turns out, I was getting upgraded. "Mr. Cole, here's your new boarding pass. You've been upgraded to first class, seat 5A. We'll be boarding in just a few minutes." For many, this is a dream come true. At no extra cost and without any effort, I had been offered a luxury experience, a chance to get a better seat with better service, to escape the near traumatic endeavor that is sitting in the middle seat of economy class on a long flight. It was an opportunity of a lifetime. And I turned it down.

Standing there in my Franciscan habit—*a sign of my vow of poverty and renunciation of the world*—I knew that there was absolutely no way that I was going to fly first class. That is not the sort of image we want circulating on the internet, let me tell you! Even if I hadn't been in my habit, there's just something unsettling about a disciple of a man nicknamed the *poverello*, "little poor man," enjoying an upgraded seat in the front while the majority of people sit uncomfortably in the back. Francis told his brothers that they were forbidden to ride horses, a convenience only afforded to the rich in his time, and one has to think that this is a fair modern equivalent. Politely, I looked at the gate attendant with a smile and said that I was happy with the middle seat that I had and that I would like to decline the upgrade.

As someone who wears my habit in airports, I'm used to getting funny looks from time to time, but hers might forever qualify as the most memorable. At first, she didn't say anything, confused at what had just happened. Once she collected herself, her puzzled look shifted to suspicion, and then to annoyance. "You don't . . . *want* the upgrade?" No doubt, this was the first time she had ever experienced this, and she didn't know how to react. She said very little, almost like she was *offended*, as if I had rejected *her*. When I saw the way she looked at me, something told me she was thinking, *What, you think you're better than me?*

Obviously, I have no idea what she was thinking, and her reaction may simply have been motivated by the fact that she now had to do additional work to switch things back. It's possible. But maybe not. The reason that my mind went to where it did—why I think there was a part of her that was legitimately offended—is that I had rejected something that she clearly valued as important and desirable. And when you reject something that is important and desirable to another, showing that you are happier *without* it, what does that say of them and their values? The rejected can't help but feel defensive.

It's experiences like these that help me understand why Christians in the early Church were so reviled and persecuted. At the time, the world had never seen anything as incredible as the Roman Empire. Spanning more than nearly 1.7 million square miles and amassing roughly a fifth of the earth's known population, it was, by the world's standards, the most marvelous kingdom that had ever existed. Its army provided power to rule peoples with force. Its economy yielded wealth and luxury found nowhere else in the world. Its lavish banquets (even if more fetishized in art than realized in practice) encouraged the excess indulgence of desire in the dining room and bedroom alike. Its politics, renowned for decorum and ingenuity, transformed cities into a kingdom that no one would ever want to leave. The Romans were proud of what they had created and sought to share their culture with the world. This was not just a first-class ticket, it was a first-class world.

And Christians rejected it.

Despite having what appeared to be all that anyone could desire at their fingertips, Christians fasted multiple times a week and offered great penances. They refused to serve in the military. They sought no political power and largely disengaged from normal city life; instead of attending banquets and bathhouses, they met early in the morning, in secret, to sing and share a simple meal. When the male head of a Roman household chose to discard a newborn child—a common and accepted practice in the ancient world—Christians would retrieve the child and raise it in their own households. In so many ways, the world had offered them a gift and Christians turned it down, living in an almost entirely contrary way. And they did so with a smile. "Oh, no thank you, we're much happier living in a different way." Not only did Christians reject the world of their neighbors, but they showed themselves to be more content without worldly wealth and power than most did with those things. Although Christians rarely spoke out directly in protest against the empire, their very lives served as a constant rebuke of the world they lived in, their presence in society a silent condemnation of their neighbors' values.

When this happens—when the world offers you what it thinks is important and desirable and you turn it down—how do you think the world is going to respond? As we saw, not favorably. The Christians had to be eliminated. Over the course of a few centuries, the Roman Empire tried repeatedly to squash out the new cult. The early Christians became the subject of a world's wrath, suppressed and tortured for what they believed and refused to do. Lawrence was grilled to death. Eulalia was rolled down a hill in a barrel filled with knives. Many were thrown to lions or beheaded. Maybe most gruesome of all was the bloody flaying to death of Bartholomew. Although the Christians were never universally or systematically executed, when the empire sought to destroy them, it showed no mercy.

And yet, once again, this is a sign of being blessed according to Jesus. As with the other Beatitudes, there would appear to be absolutely no earthly benefit to such treatment, but he looks to those who endure horrendous afflictions and says that this should be an occasion of great *joy* to all disciples. For the nonbeliever, it is nonsense. For the Christian, nothing could be more straightforward.

Reading the words of the early saints reveals that persecution was welcomed and martyrdom was all they wanted. For them, dying for the faith was a blessing that one could only hope to receive—a gift, in fact, compared to what one had to endure waiting for it to happen. To be persecuted for one's faith was not an affliction to endure but an indication that one's life was so authentically Christian that it was perceived as a threat by the world. Persecution proved that when tested in the most extraordinary way possible, the believer's faith did not fail. It confirmed that they were not meant for a world in which sin and debauchery reigned, but were instead destined to live in the kingdom of heaven.

For those who had been baptized in Christ and made disciples of his way of life, the fruits of this earth were not their true reward; the world was not their home; the Roman Empire was not their kingdom. They knew that there was absolutely nothing that the world could offer them that would truly satisfy, that it was a fading reality awaiting the coming of a new heaven and new earth. They did not love the world, for how could they? Instead, they pointed their focus beyond it, undeterred by the passing temptations offered them. There was nothing they desired more than to live in the kingdom of heaven with their Lord Jesus Christ and they were willing to endure any trial and sacrifice to get there, even if it meant giving up their lives.

At its most fundamental level, this is the essence of the Beatitudes. In every word Jesus speaks, he tries to instill in the disciples an unwavering commitment to the kingdom of heaven that nothing can shake. In each case, he points their attention to the future, reminding them of the reward that they will receive for remaining faithful, but the reward is always a piece of the same ultimate prize: a place with him in heaven. Riches, happiness, independence, food, individualism, acclaim, revenge—the world offers us all of these things with the promise of contentment and satisfaction, but Jesus knows that none of these things will ever be enough. There is nothing in this world, *not even one's life*, that could ever compare with the unfathomable fullness of the kingdom. True disciples forgo these worldly pleasures because they know what awaits them, and thus it is the confidence of possessing what the world cannot offer that makes them blessed in the here and now. When you know that is where you're going, how can you help but feel overjoyed, even while suffering?

Maybe even more important, when you possess the promise of everlasting life within you, how can you keep that to yourself? Looking to a world that gives in to debauchery, that puts its trust in riches, happiness, independence, food, individualism, acclaim, revenge—that resigns itself to a life of division or despair—how can we sit idly by and *not* reject the "gift" that is offered to us? It may be freely given and loved by the world, but it is a life that should not appeal to us. We reject it first and foremost as a condition of Gospel life, but this can hardly be separated from our call to evangelize the world. Jesus didn't come merely to save us. He doesn't give us a gift so that we will hold it to ourselves. He calls us and sends us forth so that we may witness to the world what we have found, namely, that Christ has brought eternal life through his life, death, and resurrection.

How interesting it is, then, when we come to realize that in Greek the word for "witness" is the same word used for "martyr." For the early Christians, the two were inseparable: to witness as Christ commanded was to lay down one's life. In being willing to die for their faith, they acted not merely for themselves, but for their persecutors and all that might remember their example after their death. It was a final, desperate plea to this world, to convince it of its wrongdoing and to inspire conversion, to show in the most dramatic way possible that there is something better than this world has to offer. Not even the fear of suffering and death could stop them. They loved nothing more in all of existence, and they were willing to do anything to make sure others knew about it.

When Jesus speaks of the persecuted being blessed, this is what he means. It is not the pain that they endure or the gruesome death that they face, but the unbridled love for God and neighbor that causes it to be. Those who wished to avoid persecution were entirely within their power to make that happen—all they had to do was renounce their faith, give up their practice, and the Romans would have set them free unharmed. But they didn't. Those who were persecuted received what they did precisely because they loved God more than they feared pain, and they wanted the world to know about it. Their deaths are a symbol not just of their faith, but of their desire to instill faith in those who yet trust in other gods. Blessed are those who witness to what truly matters, for their reward will be great in heaven.

When the Fall Is All There Is

In one of the social studies courses I took in high school, our teacher had us follow a current-events story about high schoolers organizing a protest. Admittedly, I have forgotten many of the details, so what I share may not be precisely what happened, but a general retelling will suffice to make my point. Apparently, the school administration had made a decision that some of the students didn't like. In response, the students decided to organize a protest, skipping class and barricading themselves in the lobby of the school until the decision was changed. There was definitely a sense, in the way I remember the coverage of the story, that the students felt that they were carrying on the legacy of the civil rights movement, standing up for something important through civil disobedience. In their eyes, the administration was wrong, and they refused to have any part of it.

Had that been the end of the story, it might have been an inspiring lesson to young people about the power of their own agency—that even though they were not adults, they could effect change. Unfortunately for them, that is not how their protest ended. Because those in administration *were* adults, they exercised their authority over the students by warning them of potential consequences: any classes missed would count against the students' attendance, resulting in a grade reduction, then suspension; athletes were unable to practice or compete if they missed class because of the protest; students caught trespassing on school property would be barred from special events like prom and pep rallies; and so on. None of it was particularly over-the-top, and all of it had to have been expected by the students. I'm not sure how the original issue was resolved, but eventually, the students returned to class, proud of the influence they had exercised, and the protest came to an end.

And then the punishments were issued. Those who missed class actually *did* lose points on their grades. Some students were suspended; athletes were benched. These are the usual consequences for skipping class, and so no one should have been surprised. But the students were. They played the victim. They complained that they were being mistreated, that they were being persecuted, that they deserved justice.

My teacher, all too happy to play the "kids these days" game, ranted about how the activists of the civil rights movement knew that their actions had consequences and showed heroism as they endured those consequences, while my generation wanted to be revolutionaries without paying for it. He called out the students for their sense of entitlement, thinking that they could stand up to the school administration and then expect to go about their lives as normal. Commitments require sacrifice, he said. Actions have consequences. You can't stand up against the powers that be and then complain when those same powers act against you. Be a revolutionary or remain comfortable, but you can't do both.

The point of the story for me, and what I think it reminds us Christians today, is that there's a big difference between being a martyr for Christ and having a martyr complex. While I don't want to judge the motivations of the students in this story, it seems to me that, at some point along the way, righteously motivated people can lose sight of the mission they set out to accomplish, and begin to care a bit too much about their own livelihoods. People like these can be found throughout popular Christianity. I think of the sad dichotomy that exists in us at times when we want to wear the crown of martyrs without having to bear the weight of the Cross. As I mentioned in the previous chapter, there are times when we want to stand up to the world while at the same time being liked by it. This will always fail to witness to the Gospel.

In my estimation, this is the driving force of Twitter. After a tweet that was intended to be prophetic receives an onslaught of critical reactions, the original poster too often shifts their attention to the negative feedback itself, highlighting the hatred of their enemies in order to be consoled. They want to be provocative but still comforted, stand with Christ but shielded from persecution. They took the first step toward martyrdom, proclaiming what was unpopular and showing that their faith is more important than public acclaim, but then undermined it by cashing in their persecution for sympathy points. As Jesus points out in his list of woes found in the Lucan Beatitudes, they have received their reward.

I know that I am guilty of this, on Twitter and among my friends. How many times have I complained about the negative things people say about me! Sometimes, of course, their words are downright hateful, and so the attention I give them is meant as a means of correction and to model a different way of interacting, but this is not always the case. Sometimes, the responses I receive are the natural conclusion of sticking my head into a hornet's nest and I have only myself to blame. Sometimes, the fact that I am being persecuted for the sake of Christ is exactly what I need to remember, but I run from it. I cower from criticism, seek out sympathy, even hide from my responsibility to

announce the kingdom because I know that it's going to bring
me personal trouble. Concerned more about how I feel and
what others will say about me, wanting to appear as a Christian
without being willing to walk as a Christian does, I fail at times
to bear witness to the Gospel in the world.

At other times, our witness suffers from the opposite problem. Rather than seeking comfort from the world, some of us
have a tendency to confuse Gospel life with countercultural
life, steadfast faith with contrarianism. Like the hipsters who
hate everything that is popular and define their lives by what
the world isn't, there are definitely Christians who are motivated more by a desire to be *against* the world than to be *for* the
kingdom. Believe it or not, these motivations are not equivalent.

As much as the world is fraught with distorted desires and
seeks false gods, not everything found outside the Church is
inherently bad. How could it be? If we believe that God is the
creator of all that is and that he mediates his presence in and
through the material world, then there is nothing outside of his
control. Neither the natural world nor the secular human world
is exempt from the possibility of carrying out his will. Scripture
reminds us that Rahab, a Canaanite woman, feared God and
protected the Israelite men sent by Joshua. The Persian king
Cyrus, a man described by Isaiah as "his anointed" (Is 45:1), was
used by God to execute his commands and exact justice upon
unfaithful Israel. When Paul preached in Athens, he noticed
an altar in one of the shrines dedicated "To an Unknown God"
(Acts 17:23), showing that they worshipped what we believe
even before it could be proclaimed to them. There in the outside
world, growing entirely outside of our influence, are truth and
reverence for God.

While we as the Church hold that we are the recipients of
the *fullness* of God's truth, we have never proposed that we are
its *only* adherents. The natural sciences reveal important facts of

creation not evident by faith, and truth is also present in other religions and cultures. "The Catholic Church rejects nothing of what is true and holy in these religions," teaches the Second Vatican Council in *Nostra Aetate*. In his papal encyclicals, Pope Francis has repeatedly reminded the world of the beauty that can be found in indigenous cultures, that there is something true about them that is not explicitly captured in the deposit of faith. To dismiss all that exists outside of the walls of the Church, to stand against the world as a defining feature of one's life, inevitably rejects that which God hopes to reveal in and through the world. Our Church has no room for blanket contrarians.

Rather, as witnesses to the Christian life, we must remember that we stand against the evils of the world and accept whatever persecution comes from it not because we hate the world in itself and want to condemn it, but because we hope to convert it. It should be our greatest desire to find that there are things in the world that *are* true, that the world, without even knowing it, *does* seek the kingdom of God, albeit by a different name. Our commitment to the Gospel compels us to reject all that is false, regardless of the personal consequences we may suffer as a result, but it also necessarily means identifying that which is true in the world in order to draw people closer to it. The most effective missionaries are not those who tear down the culture they encounter, but those who build upon the truth that already exists within it.

Those who fail to recognize even the possibility that truth exists in the world will always live with a martyr complex—suffering persecution precisely because they go looking for it. Unable to find goodness in those they oppose, failing to care for the soul of their supposed persecutor, they look for battles and seek out enemies. Unlike the early martyrs that did all they could to bring peace to the world and only accepted death as a last resort, there are Christians today who want to be persecuted so that they can use it as a weapon against others. For them, it is not a moment of inner peace before God, a sign of one's faithfulness to the kingdom; it is justification to wage war on all those who are hostile to the Church, warranting swift retaliation.

Needless to say, this undermines the very witness of martyrdom. Rather than acting differently from the world, returning love for hate, showing that our love for the kingdom of heaven is greater than anything in this life, this type of witness gives the world the only thing that it knows, violence, a desperate plea to save our own lives. Acting in this way does not break the cycle of violence, nor does it point to anything beyond.

The power of martyrdom—really, the power of our entire faith—is that death is not the end. As much as our world would say otherwise, we know that there are far worse things in this world than death, and far better things than earthly life. We lay down our lives without a care because they mean nothing next to the kingdom we will inherit. Nothing is worth losing the hope that we've found. Thus, when we come to the end of our pilgrimage, especially when it comes at the hands of our enemy, it matters how we fall. It matters how we treat our persecutor. As Prince Richard says in the 1968 film *The Lion in Winter*, just before he is to be executed, "When the fall is all there is, it matters." To go out swinging, attacking our enemy with judgments and condemnations in a futile attempt to put us back on top, betrays the very faith we claim to be dying for; we fall, but with one hand clinging to our enemy's neck. The one with true faith falls with an inner peace that cannot be shaken. They know that they have been faithful to the end, and have done everything in their power to share their faith with those who do not believe.

This is what it means to be a witness. It's not about suffering in itself or seeking a grim death; it's about having a love for God and neighbor that so far exceeds the fear of death that we would happily give our lives as a sign for those who do not yet believe.

It's about being so enflamed with the truth of the Gospel that we cannot bear the thought of anyone not knowing what we've found, even our enemies. We are compelled to do something heroic, emboldened to endure something painful. When all we can think about is making our lives a sign of the coming kingdom, forfeiting even our lives to make it known, we are on the way of Beatitude.

Questions for Reflection

1. Does your life reflect the values of the world or challenge them? Outside of Sunday services, if the government were persecuting Christians today, would there be enough evidence to convict you? Would those in power feel threatened enough by your life to care?

2. In what ways does your life invite others to hope? Do you live in a way that causes people to stop and think about their own life decisions?

3. How do you respond when you're insulted? Do you care about your attacker? Do you ever consider how your reaction might be a witness to others of our Christian life?

Practical Acts of Witness

*   When you go out into the world, imagine that everyone knows who you are and that you are a Christian. Realize that you are setting an example for the faith, and that you might be the most influential person in shaping what someone thinks about Christianity.

*   The next time you experience a personal injustice—an extra charge on a bill, being given the wrong order, forced to endure terrible service—focus intently on remaining patient

and calm. Remind yourself that, in the grand scheme of things, it doesn't matter. The way you treat the customer-service representative or the restaurant server is far more important than whatever you've been cheated from.

• As you encounter non-Christians or even anti-Christians, try to find something good and true about their lives. In your interactions with them, do everything you can to connect with and affirm the presence of God in them.

CONCLUSION
ON THE WAY TO BLESSEDNESS

A few years ago I made a video on YouTube titled "5 Words a Christian Shouldn't Say." The purpose of the video was not to go on a moral crusade of purity, outlining offensive words society already deemed inappropriate, but to draw people's attention to the ways in which our casual language unwittingly betrays our faith. There are words that we use, either flippantly or in the wrong context, that contradict what we really believe. The list included "deserve," "mine," "evil," and "unforgivable," all words that would be difficult for a Christian to argue against, and one word that might seem impossible for many to understand: "blessed." Impossible, that is, for someone who hasn't just completed this book.

In our world, the word "blessed" is used often by Christians in daily life. People share that they are blessed to have such a great family. When complimented on having a beautiful house, earning a comfortable living, or being in good health, someone may respond, "We're so blessed." For most, it is a means of expressing thanksgiving, of praising God for the gifts they possess and the happiness they enjoy in life. I have never heard someone use the word "blessed" with any malicious intent, and so my purpose in including it on my list was not to be harsh toward those who use the word regularly. I know that it comes from a good place.

But now you've just read a book on the Beatitudes, particularly a book on the Beatitudes seeking to respond to a divided and despairing world, and I hope that you see the discomfort I have with this. We've looked at what Jesus considers blessed, we've outlined what the way of Beatitude looks like, and it has left us with a problem: Jesus does not use earthly happiness as a measure of favor with God. In fact, his words suggest the very opposite.

It should go without saying that having nice things is nowhere close to the supreme blessing of God. Many people have great families, beautiful homes, well-paying jobs, and good health without any care for God and the kingdom of heaven; some even possess these things precisely *because* they have chosen to live fundamentally against God's intentions—by cheating their neighbor, attacking their enemy, and ensuring that society continues to benefit them over others. Conversely, if earthly happiness was a sign of God's favor with us, we would necessarily have to conclude that people without these things—the poor, sick, and lonely—are *not* blessed, which is a complete contradiction of Jesus's own words. When earthly happiness and blessing come to mean the same thing, something has gone terribly wrong. While I do not deny the fact that God cares for his people and often lavishly bestows gifts upon us that we do not deserve, there is definitely a sense that our view of the kingdom of heaven is filtered through our values of an earthly, secular life. Something essential about our approach to life in God has to change.

If you take anything away from this book, take this: only those who recognize the inbreaking of the kingdom of heaven in the present moment and give themselves entirely to it will truly know what it is to be blessed. It has nothing to do with eating or drinking, possessing or giving, power or weakness, praise or ridicule, success or failure. What matters is whether or not these things orient us completely and wholeheartedly toward God. What matters is that our commitment to the mission of Christ is so unwavering that we feel his presence in everything we do, transforming even afflictions into experiences of grace.

Our world is teeming with division and despair, and if this world was all we had, we might be tempted to give in to outrage or apathy. Without the hope we find in Christ, we could look at the ways our politicians harm the world, how our friends and family disappoint us, how unbridled greed corrupts our culture, and quickly choose a side. But we are not those people. The worth of our lives is not measured in money or comfort, happiness or praise. We don't have to win every argument. We don't have to fight for every dollar. We don't have to defend our honor, end world hunger, solve decades-old wars, or ensure that every person lives in peace and harmony in order for our lives to be worthwhile. As Christians, we know what we seek is not only beyond our ability, but beyond even our comprehension. That is the source of our hope. Through it all, we hold fast to the fact that God is in control.

And so, we go forth. We need not live with the intention of saving the world in all its division and despair, but we are definitely tasked with the straightforward goal of living with hope. Having felt God's loving embrace in our afflictions and having seen the inbreaking of the kingdom before our eyes, we go forward in our daily lives—in our interactions with strangers online, in the way we talk with difficult friends and family members, in dealing with the sufferings of this world—with a desire to show the world that there is another way: the way of Beatitude.

Fr. Casey Cole, OFM, is a Franciscan priest, author, speaker, and online evangelist at the popular YouTube channel Breaking in the Habit. He lives in Macon, Georgia, where he serves as chaplain to St. Peter Claver Catholic School, Mount de Sales Academy, and Mercer University. He is the author of *Called* and *Let Go*.

Cole earned his bachelor's degree from Furman University and did his priestly studies at The Catholic University of America and Catholic Theological Union.

breakinginthehabit.org
Facebook: CaseyOFM
Twitter: CaseyOFM
Instagram: CaseyOFM
YouTube: BreakingInTheHabit, UponFriarReview

AVE MARIA PRESS

Founded in 1865, Ave Maria Press,
a ministry of the Congregation of
Holy Cross, is a Catholic publishing
company that serves the spiritual and
formative needs of the Church and its
schools, institutions, and ministers;
Christian individuals and families; and
others seeking spiritual nourishment.

———◦◦◦———

For a complete listing of titles from

Ave Maria Press

Sorin Books

Forest of Peace

Christian Classics

visit avemariapress.com